HIGH EMOTIONAL INTELLIGENCE FOR MANAGERS

Effective Professional Growth Strategies for Rapid Results and Management Success at Work

ROBERT MOMENT

HIGH EMOTIONAL INTELLIGENCE FOR MANAGERS
Copyright © 2021 by Robert Moment

All rights reserved. No part of this book may be reproduced, distributed, or transmitted in any form or by any means, including recording, photocopying, or other electronic or mechanical methods, without the prior written permission of the author, except in the case of brief quotations embodied in reviews and certain other non-commercial uses permitted by copyright law.

ISBN-13:9798510680577

LIABILITY/WARRANTY

The views and interpretations expressed in this book are the authors, and are not intended to provide exact or specific advice. The author shall not be liable for any loss or damage incurred in this process of following the advice presented in this book.

CONTENTS

Introduction 7
Chapter 1: Managing Emotion 10
   Emotions in the Workplace 11
   Managing Emotions as a Manager 11
   Improving Emotional Intelligence At Home 15
   Managing Employee Emotions 16
Chapter 2: Perceiving Emotions 19
   Your Own Emotions Effect Your Perception of Emotions 21
   Perceiving Emotions and Emotional Intelligence 22
Chapter 3: Self-Awareness 24
Chapter 4: Focused Listening 27
   Focused Listening Strategies 28
Chapter 5: Facilitating Thinking Using Emotions 32
   Using Emotions to Facilitate Thinking 33
Chapter 6: Developing High Emotional Intelligence 36
   Identifying Emotional Intelligence Strengths and Weaknesses 37
   Improving your Emotional Intelligence in the Workplace 39
Chapter 7: Building Successful Workplace Teams Using Emotional Intelligence 42
   Developing an Action Plan for High Team EQ 47
Chapter 8: Adapting to Change Using Emotional Intelligence 51
   How Emotional Intelligence will Help You Manage Change 51
   Emotional Intelligence Strategies to Deal with Organizational Change 54

Chapter 9: How to Deal with Adversity Using Emotional Intelligence 57
The Relationship Between AQ and EQ 58
Dealing with Failure Using Emotional Intelligence 58

Chapter 10: How to Give Employee Feedback Using Emotional Intelligence 61
Emotionally Intelligent Feedback Checklist 64
Examples of Emotionally Intelligent Feedback 65

Chapter 11: Managing Different Personality Types 69
How to Manage Different Personality Types 69
Case Study: Conflicting Personality Types 78
Communicating with Different Personality Types Using Emotional Intelligence 79
Using Emotional Intelligence in All Communication 83

Chapter 12: The Power of Empathy 86
Strategies to Create Empathy in the Workplace 89
The Emotionally Intelligent Empathy Management Formula™ 91

Chapter 13: Managing Diversity and Inclusion Using Emotional Intelligence 93
Benefits of Diversity and Inclusion in the Workplace 94
The Relationship Between Emotional Intelligence and Diversity and Inclusion 95
Your Role in Building Workplace Diversity and Inclusion 97

Chapter 14: Handling Sensitive Workplace Communication and Situations 102
8 Tips to Handling Sensitive Workplace Situations 104
Case Study: Addressing Hygiene Issues with An Employee 106

Chapter 15: Dealing with Team Conflict and Toxic Workplace Culture Using Emotional Intelligence .. 109
Using the Four Pillars of Emotional Intelligence to

Improve Team Dynamics 109
Strategies to Improving Team Dynamics 111
Chapter 16: Communicating with Flexibility and Authenticity 115
Communicating with Different Communication Styles 115
The Importance of Authentic Communication.............. 116
Tips to Communicating with Flexibility and Authenticity 117
Chapter 17: Individual Emotional Intelligence Exercises 119
Exercise 1: Emotional Triggers 119
Exercise 2: The Purpose of Emotions 121
Exercise 3: Underlying Emotions..................................... 123
Exercise 4: Identify Your Strengths.................................. 124
Exercise 5: How to Work Through Your Emotions........ 125
Chapter 18: Team Emotional Intelligence Exercises .. 127
Exercise 1: Accepting Emotions.. 127
Exercise 2: Making Eye Contact 128
Exercise 3: Circle of Support 130
Exercise 4: Praise and Recognition 131
Exercise 5: Same Experience, Different Perspectives 132
Conclusion.. 134
Special Reader Request!.. 136
About the Author.. 137
Appendix... 138
Emotional Intelligence Assessment................................. 138
Works Cited 144

INTRODUCTION

If you had to define a great manager, what traits or skills would they possess?

Now, think of the best manager you have ever had. What made this manager so special? What did they do or what traits did they possess that makes them standout against the rest?

When we think about what makes a manager great, we often consider their "leadership skills," a term that often lumps together a multitude of important skills. Although analytical skills, technical skills, and intelligence may come to mind, one of the most critical skills a leader can have is a high level of emotional intelligence. When you thought of the best manager you ever had, it likely wasn't their savvy Microsoft Excel skills that impressed you, but their high level of emotional intelligence.

"The most effective leaders are all alike in one crucial way: They all have a high degree of what has come to be known as emotional intelligence. It's not that IQ and technical skills are irrelevant. They do matter, but… they are the entry-level requirements for executive positions."

This is what the *Harvard Business Review* wrote when they quoted renowned emotional intelligence expert Daniel Goleman (Ovans, 2015). As a manager, it is your job to bring out the best in your team, and you won't be able to do that until you bring out the best in yourself.

Simply speaking, emotional intelligence is your ability to understand and control your emotions as well as the emotions of others. This book will go into this in greater detail on what emotional intelligence entails and teach you how to increase and utilize emotional intelligence in the workplace. By increasing your own emotional intelligence as well as your teams, you will:

- **Become a better coach and motivator.** DDI, a global leadership development firm, reported that leaders with a high level of empathy (an aspect of emotional intelligence) are 40% more effective at decision-making, coaching, and engaging others (Ovans, 2015).

- **Be more productive (and so will your team!).** Emotional intelligence has been found to increase productivity and performance. *Why?* Because trusted, happy, and engaged employees are more innovative, loyal, and collaborative. Research has shown that 90% of top performers have high levels of emotional intelligence (TalentSmartEQ).

- **Keep top-performing employees and attract promising new talent.** A high turnover rate is a direct reflection of management. Studies have shown that employees don't choose to leave an organization; they decide to leave their manager. Managers with high emotional intelligence see a 62% reduction in turnover.

- **Be more successful.** Whether you are looking to exceed financial targets or have your eye on a promotion, those with a high level of emotional intelligence are more successful. A study of UC of Berkeley PhDs found that emotional intelligence is 400% more powerful than IQ when it comes to predicting success.

- **Be more profitable**. The relationship between money and emotional intelligence is undeniable. US businesses lose between $5.6 and 16.8 billion due to a lack of emotional intelligence training. Further, those with a high level of emotional intelligence outperform revenue targets by up to 20%.

Through this book, you will learn proven personal development strategies, team-building exercises, and feedback techniques rooted in emotional intelligence that you can start using today. You'll learn how to use empathy, work with different personality types and foster a diverse and inclusive workplace.

Before beginning, I recommend turning to the Appendix and completing the Emotional Intelligence Assessment. This will provide you with a better understanding of your current level of emotional intelligence. As you go through each chapter, start putting the strategies and techniques into practice. After completing this book, return to the Emotional Intelligence Assessment and see how far you have come. Like any skill, you have the power to strengthen your emotional intelligence.

CHAPTER 1
MANAGING EMOTION

Have your emotions ever gotten the best of you?

Perhaps you had a heated disagreement with a colleague or were disappointed in a team member who was late to a meeting, and you said things you later regretted.

Many triggering situations can occur in the workplace. These situations create an emotional response that you, as a manager, need to control.

Emotional responses are natural; they happen to everyone, and the fact that you experience emotions is a sign of emotional intelligence. However, to be an effective manager, you must be able to manage them.

There is an excellent analogy for controlling our emotions that Nobel Prize winner Daniel Kahneman inspired. Kahneman describes the mind as consisting of two systems. System 1 is our emotions, snap reactions, and habits, where System 2 is our rational thinking and our ability to manage emotions.

The relationship between the two systems has been described as an elephant and a rider. System 1, your raw emotions, is like an elephant. The elephant is extremely powerful and could trample a car if it had free range.

System 2 is the rider that controls the elephant and guides it in the right direction, so no cars are trampled along the way.

You need to ensure your elephant has a rider. This is crucial for work relationships and well as your decision-making, productivity and performance. After all, those with high emotional intelligence make more money and are more likely to be promoted (Winter, 2018).

Emotions in the Workplace

An emotionally intelligent organization will encourage employees to be themselves and creates a safe space for emotional expression within the office. This is great and exactly how it should be; however, it also requires a great deal of emotional intelligence.

Emotions affect how people work, collaborate, communicate and contribute to company objectives. Employees and managers must be able to handle the feelings of others as well as their own.

Managing Emotions as a Manager

Managers, especially entry-level or mid-level people managers, can experience a lot of pressure and deal with negative emotions from all angles. According to a survey, managers negative feelings stem from (Alison Robins, 2021):

- The pressure you put on yourself as a manager
- Difficult situations with employees

- Difficult situations with your boss
- Difficult situations with other managers

Sometimes, you can experience issues in all these areas at the same time. If you don't control these emotions, it can lead to emotional outbursts that negatively affect your work relationships. To prevent this from happening, here are 6 strategies you can use to manage negative emotions at work.

1. Deep breathing and mindfulness techniques

When you feel negative emotions like stress, anger, or frustration rising, take a few moments to focus on your breathing. If you can, go somewhere private or close your office door. Take 10 deep breaths, focusing on each inhale and exhale.

The following is a great mindfulness technique that involves visualizing a light illuminating the sides of a triangle with each breath.

- Inhale for 4 seconds and visualize a light traveling down one side of the triangle
- Hold your breath for 4 seconds as the light travels along the base of the triangle
- Exhale for 4 seconds as the light travels up the other side of the triangle

This technique encourages mindfulness, as your mind will be preoccupied counting your breath and visualizing the

Managing Emotion

triangle. Further, your breathwork will slow your heart rate and make you feel calmer.

2. Give yourself time to cool down

You want to respond to events and people with intention, not simply react based on emotion. If a stress inducing communication comes your way give yourself time to cool down. Avoid responding to emails, phone calls, or making big decisions when in a negative emotional state. If you find yourself in the midst of a situation where negative emotions start to rise, apply the 10-second rule. Try to distract yourself and count to 10. Although it may not get rid of the negative emotions altogether, it can help you compose yourself and gain control.

If you can excuse yourself from the situation and take some time to yourself, do it. Go for a walk or grab lunch from your favorite take-out spot. Removing yourself from the situation will allow you to cool down and respond rationally. Wait to send that reply or text until you are in a better headspace; otherwise, you may end up regretting it.

3. Know your triggers

When you are aware of your emotional triggers, you are better equipped to identify your emotional responses. Knowing your triggers will help you prepare yourself, remain calm and respond with intention when a triggering situation occurs. Identifying your triggers and these emotional responses will give you control over how you respond.

4. Learn to express emotions in appropriate ways

Managing your emotions doesn't mean you should suppress them. You must allow yourself to feel your emotions, but they must be expressed in appropriate ways. For example, if you feel angry, slamming your office door or shouting is not an appropriate way to express this.

Instead, use the advice here to take some time to cool down, examine your triggers, and respond professionally.

5. Be Accountable for your emotions

Do you tend to blame others for how you are feeling? If so, it's time to stop. You must become accountable for your emotions and behaviors. Leaders with low levels of emotional intelligence will blame others for making them feel a certain way and acting out of emotion. You are in control of your emotions and the only one who is responsible for them.

6. Write it out

If there is an office conflict or situation that continues to trouble you, write it out. Write out the problem you are having, the outcome you would like to see, and different ways you can to handle this situation. Following this, write out how you think the other person would respond and how they feel about this conflict.

7. Increase your emotional resiliency

Do you easily feel overwhelmed, or are you quick to anger? If you experience negative emotions easily, you may need to build up your emotional resiliency, so these negative emotions don't come up so quickly. Emotional resiliency will allow you to handle stressful situations and make important decisions more effectively.

8. Develop a positive mindset
People who have a high level of emotional intelligence also have a positive mindset. A positive mindset is more optimistic and is able to regulate emotions and recognize the emotions of others. Having a positive mindset does not mean that you suppress any negative emotions. Instead, it involves recognizing negative emotions when they come up and effectively working through them. Optimism will allow you to see more opportunities and solutions and it's much harder to be optimistic with a negative mindset.

Improving Emotional Intelligence At Home
In addition to managing emotions at work, you should continue to practice emotional intelligence habits at home. There are certain things you can do that will help you become aware and regulate your own emotions as well as others.

For example, people who exercise regularly are calmer and more in control of their emotions. Those who meet new people, socialize and focus on networking are also more in control of their emotions. Exercising your social skills is just as important as exercising your body.

An effective way to do this is through physical exercise. Although it may seem unrelated, research has found that those who regularly exercise are more emotionally resilient and in a better position to manage their emotions.

In your life, you should adopt a growth mindset. This can be applied at work and at home and will improve your emotional intelligence. A growth mindset is when you believe you are able to learn a new skill and grow as a person. It could entail learning a new software program at work or studying a new language in the evening. To improve your emotional intelligence, you must have a growth mindset.

If you need help improving your emotional intelligence – ask for it. Asking for help is a sign of strength, and those with a high level of emotional intelligence are more likely to ask for help when they need it. If you need more support from your team or your own boss, ask for it. It will create a more collaborative and supportive work environment that will pay off significantly.

Managing Employee Emotions

It doesn't matter how well you can control your own emotions; you will never be able to control the emotional responses of others. Instead, as a manager and people leader, you must be able to acknowledge their emotions, try to understand their perspective and respond accordingly. Here are 4 tips you can use when dealing with employees' emotions (Strange, 2021).

1. Allow for mistakes

You must understand that mistakes will happen. No one is perfect, and employees will make errors, and when they do, they will likely feel their own set of negative emotions.

If you criticize them or respond with hostility, this can damage your working relationship and their performance. Respond calmly, provide correction and aim to reduce negative emotions. If mistakes continue to happen, you can schedule a time to deliver emotionally intelligent feedback (which we will cover in an upcoming chapter).

2. Remain present
Employees who feel their manager is unavailable are more likely to feel undervalued and anxious. It is your job, as a leader, to be available to your team. This means connecting with employees to provide feedback, instill confidence, and build relationships.

Monthly one-on-one sessions are a great way to build rapport and use your emotional intelligence to check in. This shouldn't be a long meeting where you go over their performance; instead, set aside some time to allow them to raise any concerns, ask questions and provide you with feedback.

3. Build trust
Sharing emotions and being vulnerable requires a high level of trust. If your employees don't trust you, they are less likely to tell you how they feel. One of the easiest ways to build trust is by being vulnerable yourself. When they see you being transparent and authentic, they will feel more comfortable doing the same.

4. Be a good listener
If an employee opens up to you and is trying to tell you how they are feeling, and you aren't listening, they will shut

down. Having a manager that checks their email, texts on their phone, or looks distracted as the employee is trying to talk to them will break down communication and trust.

Whenever an employee is speaking with you, give them your undivided attention and really listen. Listening more than you talk will make employees feel heard and boost workplace culture significantly.

Remember, managing emotions does not mean suppressing them. As Sigmund Freud once said, "Unexpressed emotions will never die. They are buried alive and will come forth later in uglier ways." Although the sentiment is a bit intense, there is some truth here. Focus on channeling your emotions in productive ways that will benefit you, your team, and the organization.

CHAPTER 2
PERCEIVING EMOTIONS

Perceiving emotions is your ability to recognize and identify emotions in yourself and others. This ability involves complex biological and physiological processes that can come more easily to some than others.

Emotional perception is a sensory evaluation. Imagine you are at your desk, and an email for another colleague comes in, and you don't like the content within that email. You start to feel tightness in your chest, your face becomes warm, and your palms begin to sweat – you are angry. The question is, how quickly do you recognize this emotion?

In the workplace, you must also perceive emotions within others. Let's say you are speaking with a employee and they are giving you an update on a report. You hear a crack in their voice and a sniffle; you then see their eyes are red, and their face is blotchy as if they were crying. You then noticed a tissue balled up in their hand. In seconds your brain can put this together and see something is amiss. Are they sad? Sick? Scared?

Visual information is important. You can make assumptions based on the non-verbal cues and visual input, but it won't be the most accurate. Recent research suggests the best way to perceive another person's emotions is to listen. Really listen. And if you aren't sure or need clarification, ask questions.

According to the *American Psychological Association*, the best way to recognize emotions in others is to listen to them (American Psychological Association, 2017). A study involving five separate experiments and 1800 participants in the U.S. examined how we perceive other people's emotions. The participants were asked to interact with another person or observed an interaction between two different people. They were divided up into the following groups:

- Those that could look but not listen
- Those that could look and listen
- Those that listened to a computerized voice reading a transcript

With each experience, they found that those who *only* listened were able to identify emotions more accurately. The only exception to this was when the participants listened to a computerized voice. Even when presented with the exact words and sentences, emotion was only accurately detected from the human voice and could not be detected in the computer generated voice.

According to Michael Kraus, Ph.D., of Yale University, "Listening matters. Actually, considering what people are saying and the ways in which they say it can, I believe, lead to improved understanding of others at work or in your personal relationships."

Generally, visual perceptions can be helpful in understanding emotions, but as mentioned earlier, listening is vital. As a manager, your emotional intelligence will allow you to identify your own emotions so you can more accurately perceive others' emotions.

Your Own Emotions Effect Your Perception of Emotions

How you perceive emotions and facial expressions is a reflection of your understanding of that emotion. In a sense, your understanding of emotions is mirrored back to you.

The emotions you feel shape the emotions you perceive in others. A study published in the *Association for Psychological Science* conducted two experiments that found that participants saw a neutral face as smiling more often if it was paired with an unseen positive image (Siegel, Wormwood, Quigley, & Feldman Barrett, 2018). Our own experiences construct our perceptions. As one of the researchers explained, "we see the world differently when we feel pleasant or unpleasant."

If you feel negative emotions like overwhelm, anger, or frustration, you are more likely to view employees' feelings more negatively. For example, if you are angry and then read an email, you may consider this message negative, rude, or hostile. Alternatively, if you are in a great mood, you are more likely to perceive emotions as being more positive.

Perceiving Emotions and Emotional Intelligence

Perceiving emotions is a massive piece of emotional intelligence. Daniel Goleman, an emotional intelligence expert and author, has broken down emotional intelligence into five components:

Self-awareness

This is your ability to perceive your own emotions. Through your self-awareness, you will better understand your triggers, emotional responses, strengths, weaknesses, and behaviors.

Self-regulation

This is your ability to manage your emotions. With high levels of self-regulation, you can make sound decisions, remain in control, and never react with hostility. It will keep you accountable, resolve conflicts and remain flexible.

Motivation

Those with high levels of emotional intelligence are intrinsically motivated. External rewards like money and status aren't what drives them. They are motivated by joy, curiosity, and finding flow. This encourages them in their career and personal development. Self-motivated managers consistently work towards their goals and have high standards for their performance.

Empathy

Empathy is critical for managers and will allow you to put yourself in your employees' position to understand their emotions and perspective better. Empathetic managers are great at developing a solid team, often providing feedback and support.

Social Skills
Your social skills will help you build rapport, manage change and resolve conflict. Managers with high emotional intelligence have better social skills and are better communicators.

You need to perceive emotions, both your own and others, to have a high level of emotional intelligence. Once you can perceive them, you can then work on understanding emotion and responding appropriately.

CHAPTER 3
SELF-AWARENESS

Self-awareness is the foundation upon which emotional intelligence is built. It's your first step. Without self-awareness, you won't have self-regulation, motivation, empathy, or social skills.

By improving your self-awareness, you will be able to spot arising emotions, anticipate emotional reactions and understand your triggers. For better self-awareness and a strong emotional intelligence foundation, practice the following strategies.

1. Step outside of your comfort zone
Humans naturally tend to avoid unpleasant emotions or uncomfortable feelings. We try to repress them or avoid the situation altogether. In some cases, avoiding triggers can be effective, but when you often shove emotions out of the way, you lose your ability to identify and manage them.

For example, giving a presentation or public speaking may make you feel nervous or scared, so you avoid any opportunities that could lead to this, even if it would positively impact your career.

In the event you are put on the spot, you may react unfavorably. Slowly start stepping outside of your comfort zone and do things that make you feel uncomfortable.

Identify how you are feeling and work on managing any negative emotions that come up.

2. Write in a journal
This is one of the most effective ways to improve self-awareness and emotional intelligence as a whole. Using the example above, let's say you spoke up in a Town Hall and asked a question – something totally outside of your comfort zone. Later, journal about this experience.

- How did you feel then?
- How do you feel now?
- Why do you believe you experienced these emotions?
- Are they based on facts or fear?

Try to write in your journal every day. Write down the emotions you felt throughout the day and a specific event that triggered this. How did you respond? How did others respond? This will become a more unconscious process through repetition, and you will establish an in-depth understanding of your emotions.

3. Meditate and practice mindfulness
Meditation is an effective way to increase your self-awareness. Research has found that yoga and meditation programs intended to enhance self-awareness resulted in reduced stress, greater mindfulness, enhanced resiliency, and greater job satisfaction (Trent, et al., 2019).

Carving out a designated time without distractions will allow you to pay attention to your inner state and connect with yourself. If you are new to meditation, start with a 5 minute guided meditation. With practice, you can increase your time. This is also an effective tool for the second component of emotional intelligence, self-regulation.

4. Ask for feedback
You may view your behaviors and emotions in one way, but that may not be the reality or the way others are perceiving them. Your behaviors and moods could affect others in ways you don't realize. Asking for external feedback will help you improve your self-awareness.

Reach out to those you trust, like family and close friends, and ask them to describe you, your strengths, and your weaknesses. What they have to say may surprise you. Take this information and reflect on it.

It is important that you don't take one person's perspective as your defining qualities, but it can provide valuable insight. An increased level of self-awareness will help you boost your overall emotional intelligence and make you a more effective leader.

CHAPTER 4
FOCUSED LISTENING

Listening is critical to effective communication and leadership. It allows you to make informed decisions, display empathy, answer questions and understand instructions.

Active listening occurs when you direct your attention to listening and understanding. It involves the words being said as well as tone, gestures, facial expressions, and body language. As the listener, you may ask follow-up questions, or ask for clarification so you understand the message.

This is a type of focused listening. Focused listening is used in many different realms to increase comprehension and reduce misunderstandings. When you are speaking with someone, what are you focusing on? There are three levels of focused listening. (Balman & Bruce, 2015):

1. Self-Focused Listening
Self-focused listening is when you are more focused on your own thoughts and what is going on inside you. This can happen to the best of us if we aren't conscious of where our attention is. Instead of listening to the other person, you think about how the conversation affects you, your feelings, opinions, or reactions, and even distracting thoughts like your after-work errand list or what you want to get for lunch.

2. Relationship Focused Listening
Relationship focused listening is when you are laser-focused on the person you are speaking with. You are paying attention to every word they are saying and intently focused on them.

3. Universal Focused Listening
Universal focused listening takes your listening a step further. It goes beyond the words being spoken and includes non-verbal context, intent, environment, and atmosphere. This is a very effective form of focused listening that you can utilize with individuals, teams, and large groups of people. It involves watching facial expressions, body language, and paying attention to the emotional field. You are listening to what is said, but also what is not said.

Focused Listening Strategies
Work environments changed significantly as a result of COVID-19, with many people continuing to work remotely. This has added a unique set of challenges that can make focused listening more difficult. You don't get the same input from a Zoom meeting or email as you would an in-person conversation. The shift to remote work has diminished the listening skills for many.

Whether you are working remotely and using video conferencing or communicating face-to-face, the following techniques will improve your listening skills at work.

Maintain eye contact
When you facing the person you are speaking with and making eye contact, you are focusing your attention on that

person and what they are saying. Although you may think you can multi-task – listen, *and* send off that email and text your kids back - you are mistaken. When you divide your attention, you aren't really listening.

In Western culture, eye contact is also a sign of respect. Despite it being the norm, prolonged eye contact can be difficult for a lot of people. Shyness, shame, guilt, cultural background, or other emotions may prevent them from making eye contact with you. That's okay. You can only control your actions.

Keep your eye contact relaxed. I've seen people take this advice a little too literally and stare so fixedly at the other person they make people uncomfortable. If your gaze is too intense it can come off as intimidating. Look away now and then, but continue to face the person you are speaking with and give them your undivided attention.

Pay attention to non-verbal cues
A great deal of our communication and understanding is from non-verbal cues. Although there is some scientific debate as to how much, one famous study from Albert Mehrabian suggests that communication is 55% nonverbal, 38% vocal, and only 7% words (MasterClass, 2020). This rule suggests that even over the phone, you are getting a lot more than just words – tone, pace, and pitch provide a great deal of context, helping you understand the message.

When you face a person, you can see fatigue, disengagement, boredom, or frustration on their face. It's something you may not get from their spoken words or an email. If working remotely, video calls will provide a bit more information and improve communication, but it still isn't as rich in non-verbal cues as face-to-face communication is.

Keep an open mind and be present
Instead of listening, many people have an internal dialogue with themselves, either judging or criticizing the other person, or thinking of what they want to say next. When listening, focus on what they are saying without jumping to conclusions.

This also means avoid finishing another person's sentences. Don't assume you know what they are trying to express and rush them, attempting to finish their sentence for them. It will break down communication, throw off their train of thought and make them feel pressured.

Ask clarifying questions
If you don't understand what another person is saying or you are having trouble hearing them, ask for clarification. Misunderstandings occur when you don't ask questions and walk away from the conversation confused. If you need clarification, wait until the speaker pauses, then say something such as "Sorry, can we back up a bit. I didn't understand ... " or "what did you mean when you said ... ".

It's important to ask questions that are relevant to the conversation. If your co-worker was speaking, and you said, "Sorry, quick question, when did you get that watch? It's stunning", it would lead the conversation astray and expresses disinterest in the topic at hand.

Don't interrupt
If you have been in a meeting with several opinionated and outspoken individuals, you know how interruption will completely dismantle the flow of information.

As a manager, if you have someone on your team who interrupts others, your team's quieter members will stop speaking up. You must moderate these behaviors using your emotional intelligence and ask the 'interrupter' to allow the other individuals to finish before speaking up.

You must also ensure you aren't interrupting anyone either. If you do, you're sending messages you probably don't want to be sending like "I'm more important," "I don't have time for this," or "I don't care what you have to say." As you can imagine, this is very damaging to morale.

Use empathy
When you are speaking with someone, try feeling what they are feeling. If they tell you something sad and are crying, use your empathy to try and understand their perspective and offer your support.

Use appropriate facial expressions and match their tone. Empathy is the heart of listening. If someone is expressing frustration or stress, try to put yourself in their shoes and understand where they are coming from. You don't need to understand their experience completely to display empathy.

CHAPTER 5
FACILITATING THINKING USING EMOTIONS

There are several theories that examine emotional intelligence. One of these theories is called the Mayer and Salovey Four-Branch Model. This model was developed in 1997 and entails the following four emotion-related abilities (Brackett, Delaney, & Salovey).

1. Perception of Emotion
This is a person's ability to identify emotions in themselves and others using body language, tone of voice, and facial expressions. As we touched on in a previous chapter, those capable of perceiving emotion can better communicate emotional needs.

2. Use of Emotion to Facilitate Thinking
You can use emotion to enhance your thinking and adapt to different situations. Those who know how to use emotion to facilitate thought realize that certain emotions are better than others for target outcomes.

For example, feelings of frustration or anger would be helpful if you are about to run a race or go to a kickboxing class. When certain emotions boost adrenaline, you can use them to increase strength, stamina, and energy. On the other hand, these same emotions could hinder you if you were to sit down and study or paint. We'll touch on this in more detail shortly.

3. Understanding of Emotion
If you have a high level of emotional intelligence, you can differentiate between emotions, triggers, and reactions. For example, you know the act of losing a loved one can result in sadness, anger, and despair, and losing your keys in the morning can trigger feelings of frustration, stress, and anger.

4. Management of Emotion
This is your ability to remain open to different emotions, understand your emotions' value and function, and know how to use your emotions. Utilizing strategies like deep breathing or taking a walk to calm down before addressing an issue is an example of managing emotion. This will also provide you with greater insight into others' perspectives.

Now that you have the background knowledge, we'll examine how you can use emotions to facilitate thinking.

Using Emotions to Facilitate Thinking
Emotions are very powerful and can improve your decision-making, creativity, and reasoning. They don't have to be positive emotions either. All emotions, both positive and negative, can affect your thinking.

Positive emotions can provide you with a greater perspective and expanded thinking, increase creativity and make you more willing to explore possibilities. Negative emotions can help you focus, pay closer attention to detail and help you spot errors.

To use your emotions, you need to understand your different moods and how you typically respond. You can trigger emotions within yourself or others with the following:

Images
Social media, pictures, news – they can all impact your emotions. You can use this to inspire you, or if you aren't conscious of the images you are taking in, it can distract or discourage you. This is why some people will put up inspirational photos in their home gym, create vision boards or select particular artwork for their home or office.

Posture
Research has found that your posture and body language can affect your mood. For example, power poses, where you stand tall, arms to your side, taking up space, can make you feel more confident.

A Harvard University study conducted by Amy Cuddy found those who held a high power pose for two minutes felt more powerful and performed better in mock interviews (Carney, Cuddy, & Yap, 2010). You can use this to your advantage - when you need to feel more powerful and confident, use high-power poses.

Language
This involves both your thoughts and spoken words. What you say to yourself can impact your emotions. This is what makes affirmations so powerful and effective.

- *What words and thoughts are you having?*
- *Do you praise yourself and talk yourself up?*
- *Is your internal chatter pessimistic and negative?*

Be mindful of the language and thoughts you are having, as it can fuel your emotions.

The relationship between emotions and thoughts goes two ways. Your emotions can impact your thoughts, and your thoughts can affect your emotions. In the workplace, this can help you deliver an excellent presentation, impress your superiors, increase performance and motivate your team.

CHAPTER 6
DEVELOPING HIGH EMOTIONAL INTELLIGENCE

Emotional intelligence is a skill, and just like any other skill, it can be developed. With the increasing importance of emotional intelligence and its countless benefits, many employers are now hiring for this specific skill. In fact, a recent survey found 75% of hiring managers were more likely to promote a candidate with high emotional intelligence over one with a high IQ, and 71% said outright that they value emotional intelligence more than IQ (Bariso, 2020).

Although some candidates may get by with exaggerated Excel skills, it is much harder to fake emotional intelligence in an interview. Hiring managers can often recognize high emotional intelligence very quickly or may administer an emotional intelligence test during the hiring process.

Fortunately, it isn't a matter of having it or not. Just as you can brush up on your Microsoft abilities, you can improve your emotional intelligence. Emotional intelligence consists of various elements, as discussed in earlier chapters, and you can have strengths and weaknesses. For example, you may have a high level of self-awareness but lack empathy. Just as you can target specific Microsoft skills like improving your PowerPoint abilities, you can target your emotional intelligence weakness, like empathy, in order to have a higher overall level of emotional intelligence. Before you can improve, you must understand what your strengths and weaknesses are.

Identifying Emotional Intelligence Strengths and Weaknesses

As a people leader, you must improve your emotional intelligence in order to succeed. It can be difficult for some, especially those with low emotional intelligence, to identify their strengths and weaknesses. If you lack self-awareness, a critical element of emotional intelligence, you could struggle to understand where you fall short.

Think of any feedback you have received or where you may struggle. When you interact with others, try to assess their body language and how they respond. This can help you understand where your emotional intelligence strengths and weaknesses are.

Here is another great exercise to help (Davis). Get a piece of blank paper and draw two large circles. Within the first circle, draw a vertical and horizontal line, so the circle is divided into even quarters. Label the quarters as follows: self-awareness, self-control, social awareness, and relationship management. Just as you did with the first circle, divide the second circle into four sections but use it as a pie graph, giving the biggest slice to the aspect of your workplace emotional intelligence you think is the strongest and the second biggest slice to the element you think is the second-most developed. Continue this for all four pieces.

This exercise will give you a visual understanding of the areas you need to be focusing on. For further assessment, take the quiz in the Appendix of this book. Strengths and weaknesses can look differently, but when it comes to emotional intelligence here is what we commonly see in the workplace:

Emotional Intelligence Strengths
- Assertive
- Finds solutions quickly
- Easy communicator
- Supportive of their team and coworkers
- Fosters a low-stress working environment
- Motivates and inspires others
- Identifies the strengths and weaknesses within themselves and their team
- Makes others feel comfortable

Emotional Intelligence Weaknesses
- Uninspiring or demotivating
- Makes people feel uncomfortable
- Provides poor direction
- Does not appreciate different perspectives
- Creates a high-stress environment
- Impulsive
- Poor communicator

Everyone has weaknesses, but your overall level of emotional intelligence is increased significantly when you strengthen these weaknesses. Fortunately, there are many ways you can improve.

Improving your Emotional Intelligence in the Workplace

Understanding your EQ strengths and weaknesses will tell you where to focus your efforts and help you keep track of your improvement and growth. Now, to receive the competitive advantage and increase your emotional intelligence, practice the following strategies with your EQ strengths and weaknesses top of mind.

Practice active and focused listening

Use the strategies listed in Chapter 4 to improve your listening skills. When speaking with others, you must listen to understand rather than waiting for your turn to speak. Pay attention to nonverbal signals and contextual information as well. Those with high emotional intelligence are excellent listeners.

Foster a growth and positive mindset

First and foremost, you must have a growth mindset. You need to understand and believe that you can improve your emotional intelligence. Attitude is so important, and it will impact others and their perception of you. If you have a negative attitude, others will adjust accordingly and are more likely to match this disposition. Do what you can to get into a positive mindset, such as starting your day off with meditation, a good breakfast, or walking outdoors.

Be assertive

Assertive doesn't mean bossy or overbearing. It's a direct and honest way of communicating and can earn you respect and increase emotional intelligence. When you are assertive, you can express your needs while remaining respectful and empathetic to others.

Respond > React
Fast reactions are triggered by your emotions and not always based on fact. Although reactions can be helpful, like running from a dangerous animal, they aren't necessarily great in the workplace. Emotional outbursts fueled by anger won't serve you. Instead, you must remain calm and respond using emotional intelligence. When you are in an emotionally triggering situation or the midst of conflict, think it through and consciously choose your words and how you want to respond.

Welcome and appreciate feedback
Those with a high level of emotional intelligence appreciate and welcome feedback from others. They can assess the feedback for themselves and can adjust accordingly without letting their emotions get the best of them. If you find you get defensive, combative, angry, or hurt any time someone offers you feedback, it's time to put this in check. Take a few moments to understand where the other person is coming from and remind yourself that this feedback is not an attack on your character. When you frame feedback as an opportunity for growth, you are more likely to appreciate it.

Always utilize leadership skills
Leadership skills can be applied in all interactions, regardless of whether you are a manager or not. Your decision-

making, problem-solving, and communication skills are a reflection of your emotional intelligence. If you find you are struggling in this area, focus on developing these leadership skills and you will see that an increase in emotional intelligence follows.

Empathize with the people you work with
You must empathize with everyone you work with, regardless of position. Those who have a high level of emotional intelligence can relate to everyone on a human level. This creates an environment of mutual respect and understanding. Empathy is an essential element of emotional intelligence, and we will touch on this in greater detail in the following chapters.

All of the strategies and techniques contained within this book will help you increase your emotional intelligence. With conscious effort and practice, you can further develop your strengths and improve your weaknesses.

CHAPTER 7
BUILDING SUCCESSFUL WORKPLACE TEAMS USING EMOTIONAL INTELLIGENCE

They say a team is only as good as their leader. As a manager, what are you doing to create an emotionally intelligent team? When your team has a higher level of emotional intelligence, you will reap the benefits. In addition to managing with emotional intelligence, you can play an active role in building successful workplace teams.

Research published in the *Harvard Business Review* has uncovered the underlying processes that build successful teams. When developing your team, the researchers explained it well, "a piano student can be taught to play Minuet in G, but he won't become a modern-day Bach without knowing music theory and being able to play with heart." (Urch Druskat & Wolff, 2001) Emotional intelligence can't be faked or executed in silos. As a manager, you must create the conditions for your team to develop emotional intelligence, including trust, group efficacy, and a sense of group identity. As a leader, here is what you can do to build a successful workplace team using emotional intelligence:

1. Act as a leader
Before you can grow your team's emotional intelligence, you must cultivate the following within yourself:

- *Self-awareness:* As a leader, you must recognize your own emotions.
- *Emotional management*: As a leader, you must be able to remain cool, calm, and collected. You must be able to manage your own emotions.
- *Effective communication:* As a leader, you must be able to express your thoughts and provide clear and concise direction.
- *Social awareness:* As a leader, you must be able to recognize what's going on around you and respond accordingly.
- *Conflict resolution:* As a leader, you must be able to find appropriate solutions to conflict.

Leaders who are respected by their team will have more significant influence. Research has shown that highly respected leaders possess the following traits:

- Demonstrate a willingness to change and learn from their mistakes
- Polite and respectful to everyone
- Actively listen (universal focused listening)
- Don't make excuses
- Help others and provides support
- Keeps their word, trustworthy

2. Identify the strengths and weakness of your team

You can use the same exercise in the previous chapter to identify the strengths and weaknesses of your team. Your team is built up of unique individuals with diverse talents, skills, and knowledge. Knowing your team, their lives outside of the office, and their strengths and weakness will help you develop the group as a whole.

3. Motivate your team

One of the most effective ways for you to motivate your team is to lead by example. When your team sees that you are inspired, they are more likely to be motivated in return. You can also spark passion in your team by recognizing your team members' accomplishments and hard work, having an engaging work environment that values the contributions of everyone, and ensuring that everyone is working towards a shared goal with a greater sense of purpose.

4. Develop team norms

According to a study, "Group emotional intelligence is about small acts that make a big difference. It is not about a team member working all night to meet a deadline; it is about saying thank you for doing so. It is not about an in-depth discussion of ideas; it is about asking a quiet member for his thoughts. It is not about harmony, lack of tension, and all members liking each other; it is about acknowledging when harmony is false, tension is unexpressed, and treating others with respect." (Urch Druskat & Wolff, 2001). Establish team norms with emotional intelligence and stick to them. Norms centered around emotional intelligence like recognition and gratitude will go a long way.

5. Manage stress creatively

Unmanaged stress can lead to burnout which has physical and mental consequences. There will be elements of pressure in all workplaces, but you should create an environment to reduce it or handle it in a healthy way. There are creative ways you, as a manager, can help keep stress levels down.

Stick to a schedule: An unreliable, ever-changing schedule can contribute to feelings of burnout. Further, if you repeatedly rush or extend projects, it negatively affects your team's time management and puts them in a stressful situation that you could have avoided. If you find yourself doing this, you must focus on your own time management and planning skills, so your team doesn't suffer as a result.

Discourage multitasking: Multitasking may seem more productive, but it often results in inferior performance and can take tasks longer to be completed. Allow employees to focus on one task at a time, and it will both reduce stress and increase performance.

Encourage periods of rest: Employees that are always on edge, constantly checking emails and answering text messages will experience burnout much faster and ultimately increase your turnover rate. Even the most passionate employees need periods to rest and disconnect from work. Ensure everyone is taking breaks, and this becomes an integral part of your workplace culture.

Resolve conflicts: Conflicts can happen, and that's okay, but you need to effectively address any issues before they create a toxic work environment or lead to harassment or hostility.

Always be empathetic: Understand that your employees are people first, with lives outside of the office. For example, if someone on your team lost a loved one, you should demonstrate compassion and ask how you can best support them.

6. Allow all members to have a voice
Build your team's communication skills by working on active listening, understanding nonverbal communication, and allowing everyone the opportunity to share how they feel. Sometimes people feel like venting, and that's okay, but you should then focus on how you can constructively resolve any issues. Focus on coming up with ideas to solve the problem together. Encourage participation from quieter members of your team and ensure everyone has the opportunity to share ideas and voice their opinion.

7. Encourage work and play
Team building activities that are held outside of the office and focus on fun can bring your team together. The research has shown that employees who spend time with one another outside of the office have better working relationships. As Grant Gordon from Solomon Consulting Group said, "Whether you have a customary Friday afternoon beer with your co-workers, take the whole team to a baseball game a few times a season or sweat together in corporate challenge events, the result is the same: Colleagues who are in each other's lives work hard. You're no longer a collection of individuals who gather in an office but a true community pulling for group success." (Rampton, n.d.).

Developing an Action Plan for High Team EQ

Your action plan for developing high team emotional intelligence will be unique to your organization's needs. This plan will consist of four distinct phases; Evaluation, Training, Application, and Review.

Phase 1: Evaluation

As with any new initiative, you must prepare accordingly - find out where our team is now and where you want to be. Your action plan in phase one could consist of the following:

- Assess organizational needs
- Self-assessment
- Team assessment
- Individual assessments of members of the team
- Gather feedback
- Assign responsibilities for change
- Align company and team values to be emotionally intelligent

Phase 2: Emotional Intelligence Training

This is a vital piece of the puzzle and should be tailored to your organization. Effecting training will provide team members with a firm understanding of what emotional intelligence entails, how to improve emotional intelligence and how to use it in the workplace. Within your training, you should address the following:

- Introduction to emotional intelligence (EI) and the benefits of high EI
- The top 3 reasons you need emotional intelligence to reach your full potential.
- Taking the first step: Measuring your own emotional intelligence.
- Five emotional intelligence competencies.
- Identifying and understanding the four main components of emotional intelligence.
- Acting with empathy.
- Recognizing behaviors associated with high emotional intelligence.
- Elements of emotional intelligence including self-awareness, self-management, social awareness, and relationship management.
- Assessing your strengths and weaknesses within specific emotional intelligence elements.
- Lowering stress, finding greater happiness, and improving relationships at home and work.
- The downside of overplaying any particular emotional intelligence characteristics.
- Creating an action plan for analyzing your emotional intelligence, getting feedback from others, and taking the actions needed to enhance your sense of confidence and well-being.
- Improving communication at work and building more prosperous and more satisfying relationships.
- Analyzing various communication styles and recognizing your own.

During the training phase, your team will also participate in self-directed learning, goal setting and be provided with the opportunity to practice and receive feedback.

Phase 3: Application of Training

The skills learned in training must immediately be applied in the workplace. The transfer of knowledge will help make any newly acquired emotional intelligence skills stick. The application process may not always be perfect, and team members will make mistakes, but with practice, your team's EQ will continue to get better. During this phase, you must:

- Foster a culture that will allow emotional intelligence to thrive.
- Model emotional intelligence skills.
- Frequently encourage the use of emotional intelligence while at work.
- Remove any constraints that limit the use of emotional intelligence.

Phase 4: Review

The review phase is the time to look back at your assessments completed in phase 1 (evaluation) and see how far you've come. Developing a high emotional intelligence team won't happen overnight, so don't expect to see massive, lasting change the same week you begin. Check in on your team's progress 3 and 6 months after training, and use the same evaluation tools to see where your team's emotional intelligence level is. At the 6 month mark, consider a refresher training session or a round-table discussion of your team's progress and get a pulse check on how each team member is feeling.

CHAPTER 8
ADAPTING TO CHANGE USING EMOTIONAL INTELLIGENCE

Over the past year, we have seen a significant amount of change. When the pandemic first swept America, many businesses were forced to pivot and make changes quickly. Entire offices and client work had to be conducted remotely.

Change isn't easy, and when it happens in the workplace, it can lead to an increased burnout rate. Research has found that organizational change can mimic the grief suffered after the loss of a loved one (Henderson-Loney, 1996). That said, change is inevitable, especially in business, so you need to be able to adapt. Adapting to change is easier when using emotional intelligence.

How Emotional Intelligence will Help You Manage Change

Your emotional intelligence will be your most used tool in your professional toolbox as it applies to every situation. Research has found that 75% of careers are derailed for reasons related to emotional intelligence. This includes unsatisfactory team leadership during difficult times or an inability to adapt to change (HappyCamper, 2015).

Your emotional intelligence will help you avoid undue stress and sustain positive results and a positive team when it comes to change management. There are several ways in which your emotional intelligence will help you manage change.

It will help you make better decisions
When negative emotions are running high, the logical and rational part of your brain becomes quiet. In some cases, it can shut off entirely. This is when you become reactive, basing decisions on the way you are feeling instead of facts.

For example, if you are angry with a co-worker, you may want to shout and tell them off, but there will be long-lasting negative repercussions for this behavior. When you use your emotional intelligence skills, you can put these emotions in check and make better decisions.

It will help you be more resilient
No matter what role you play in your organization, you will encounter setbacks. It's a part of life, and sometimes you have no control over them. What you do have control over is how you respond to these setbacks.

With greater levels of emotional intelligence and using your emotional intelligence skills, you will have a better perspective and be able to see opportunities and solutions with greater clarity as negative emotions would cloud your thinking.

It will make you a better leader
A prevalent employee complaint is feeling undervalued. Employees who feel this way and are then forced to deal

with significant change don't recover as quickly. This can negatively affect their performance, engagement, and attitude.

Using your emotional intelligence, you will help temper reactions and provide a more balanced perspective for employees. Further, you will provide the support and acknowledgment that your team needs, so they are in an excellent position to pivot and accept change.

It will help you manage your stress
Stress can wreak havoc on your physical and mental health. Although stress has a function, like all other emotions, and can serve a purpose, like when you are in a life-threatening situation, it can also be over-active.

Stress has become disproportional, with many managers and corporate leaders enduring chronic stress and resulting health effects. When you are already operating with a high-stress level, change can feel unbearable.

Emotional intelligence will help you manage your stress levels through self-awareness and self-regulation so that it doesn't become chronic or lead to feelings of overwhelm.

It will help you take action
When you feel stressed, overwhelmed, or out of control, you can become paralyzed; unable to respond or make decisions. We often talk about emotions causing us to react quickly, but it can also cause us to freeze. Your emotional intelligence will give you a greater perspective and allow you to make informed decisions and take action.

There is no question that emotional intelligence will help you navigate and manage change, but you may still be wondering how to best utilize your emotional intelligence to do so. There are specific emotional intelligence strategies that you can use to help you deal with organizational change.

Emotional Intelligence Strategies to Deal with Organizational Change

As your organization introduces a significant change, use the following emotional intelligence strategies to help your team embrace it (Wiens & Rowell, 2018).

Identify the source of the resistance

If you or one of your team members feels resistant to the change, it's essential to understand why. This brings us back to the foundation of emotional intelligence – self-awareness. Asking the right questions can sometimes help identify the source of resistance.

- *Am I concerned it will impact my autonomy?*
- *Will it make me look incompetent?*
- *Will it make my work more challenging?*
- *Do I believe I won't be able to keep up?*

Having more information about the change and the reasoning for the change can help employees feel more comfortable. As a manager, provide your team with as much information as possible, being transparent and open to feedback.

If your organization is making changes to move the business in a new direction, tell your team. Being involved in change, or at the very least involved in the conversations, can give people a sense of control and reduce resistance.

Question your emotional response
Our emotions can cause us to have knee-jerk reactions and responses, and they can be based on the stories we tell ourselves rather than facts. When change occurs, it can trigger different interpretations that aren't always in line with reality. The next time you feel strong emotions after a big change, ask yourself the following questions:

- *What primary emotion am I experiencing because of this change?*
- *What do I believe to be true that is triggering this emotion?*
- *Is this based on a story I am telling myself or facts?*

This will provide you with a greater perspective. This is an effective tool to use with your team as well. Rumors will spread quickly, especially if team members aren't communicated with before the change. Allow your team to ask these questions, and if a really big change is coming, schedule in some one-on-one time to get a pulse check and address any of the emotional responses they are experiencing.

Own your role in the situation
As a self-aware manager, you must reflect on how your behaviors contribute to your team's experience of change.

If a significant change is looming, and you speak negatively about it or become noticeably stressed, your team will feel the same way.

Although transparency is important, you must check in with yourself before communicating the change to your team. Use the mindfulness techniques and exercises in this book to help you understand your own frame of mind. Understanding how your response to change can trigger a negative chain of reactions will help you be more conscious of your perspective.

Try to have a positive lookout
Research has shown that when you make an effort to have a more positive outlook, it can make you more receptive to change (Huy, 1999). To help you see the change in a more positive light, ask yourself the following questions:

- *What are the opportunities brought about by this change?*
- *How will these opportunities help me?*

As a manager, you can positively frame the change to your team by answering these questions for them. Tell your team what new opportunities will exist and how it can positively impact them and their role. Adapting to change gives you a competitive advantage as a leader. If you feel yourself resisting, refer back to these 4 strategies.

CHAPTER 9
HOW TO DEAL WITH ADVERSITY USING EMOTIONAL INTELLIGENCE

Adversity, setbacks, and failure are part of life. These circumstances are bound to show up at work, and the way you deal with them will impact your success. When faced with adversity, you have two options; you can see the challenge as a stepping stone that will bring your further, or you can see it as a roadblock that is holding you back.

Those who have a high level of emotional intelligence are better equipped to deal with adversity. These people are able to look beyond current circumstances and know they have the ability to use the situation to their advantage. High emotional intelligence individuals are able to do this because they ask themselves the right questions when faced with adversity.

- *How can this failure serve me?*
- *How can I improve going forward?*
- *What is the best, most emotionally intelligent way of dealing with it?*

Emotionally intelligent managers and teams know that adversity will strengthen their problem-solving skills, increase resilience, boost experience and help them think critically and creatively. Those with a high level of emotional intelligence consider failure to be a mental growth spurt or a crash course.

The Relationship Between AQ and EQ

The term adversity quotient (AQ) was coined in 1997 by Paul Stolz in his book *Adversity Quotient: Turning Obstacles Into Opportunities*. Your AQ determines how well you deal with life's adversities; it's your resiliency. There is a direct relationship between your ability to deal with adversity and your level of emotional intelligence. An individual with high emotional intelligence and is aware of their emotions is more resilient. The higher your emotional intelligence, the higher your AQ will be. This leads to several benefits in the corporate world.

A workforce that has both high levels of AQ and EQ is more likely to follow through and achieve goals, is more loyal, and performs better.

Dealing with Failure Using Emotional Intelligence

When we use our emotional intelligence to deal with adversity, we can actually become more successful. This is a part of control theory. This theory suggests that there is a sweet spot when dealing with our emotions after failure that will help push us to succeed. In order to access this sweet spot and use your emotional intelligence to overcome adversity, use the following steps.

1. Recognize your mistake and acknowledge failure
Failure gets a bad rap, but it is the necessary evil to become better, more experienced, and successful. The hardest part for many people is having the required level of self-awareness to acknowledge when they have made a mistake. For your brain to boost the failure-driven success skills, you need to first feel all those feelings associated with failure. To help you acknowledge these feelings, ask yourself what caused the failure and be very honest with yourself. Next, ask yourself if you could have avoided the mistake. Once you have identified the error and acknowledged that it was avoidable if you acted differently, your mental thermostat (control theory) will kick in and prevent the problem from happening again in the future.

2. Don't 'sugar coat' the failure
You may be tempted to always look for the silver lining, but this is a type of emotional rationalization that won't lead to success. In fact, research has found that in doing so, you may be preventing your improvement and could make the same mistake again (Nelson, Malkoc, & Shiv, 2017). If you mask negative feelings and try to make them positive; they may show up again later (and stronger) the next time you make a mistake. Bottom line, don't look for external factors to blame and don't excuse failure by telling yourself you aren't cut out of the task.

3. Dial into those feelings of failure and take action
This may not sound ideal but hear me out. Self-awareness and empathy are significant elements of emotional intelligence. You must show yourself empathy, as well as

others. If you feel hurt or upset over the failure or adverse situation – that's okay. You can allow yourself to feel those feelings while exhibiting self-compassion. To deal with these emotions, try and identify where they are coming from and label the negative feeling. Next, determine what this feeling is driving you to do. Failure can help push you to take positive action, and you have the power to control it. For example, if you submitted a report with an error on it, in the future, this may trigger the action to review reports more carefully before submitting them.

Use these emotional intelligence principles to successfully manage workplace adversity.

CHAPTER 10
HOW TO GIVE EMPLOYEE FEEDBACK USING EMOTIONAL INTELLIGENCE

Feedback can help a person feel supported, motivated, and equipped to do the job, or it can leave an employee feeling demotivated, discouraged, frustrated, and disengaged. You, as the manager, determine the outcome. Feedback is an essential element of a manager's job, and it will determine how happy and engaged your team is. A study found that 70% of employees perception of their workplace is a direct result of their manager's behavior and feedback (Momeni, 2009).

Emotional intelligence expert Dan Goleman has said, "great leaders can empathize with their employees and still have tough conversations about performance with them." To be emotionally intelligent, it doesn't mean you have to walk on eggshells and never provide feedback in fear of upsetting your employee. You can give direct feedback that employees will positively receive through emotionally intelligent delivery.

Whether you deliver one-time feedback on a specific task, conduct an annual review, or provide team feedback on a project, you can do so effectively so that everyone leaves feeling motivated and supported.

Providing conscious feedback delivery and getting in the right headspace.
As a manager, you shouldn't necessarily give feedback on the fly with no prior consideration or reflection. You need to check in with your emotional state before doing so. If you feel angry, frustrated, or disappointed, you should wait until you are in a better headspace. Feedback should be delivered when you are calm, in control of your emotions, and in a more positive frame of mind.

In addition to being emotionally prepared, you should also prepare what you want to say.

Emotionally intelligent feedback is clear and concise. If there are several areas to address, it may be better to break these up and deliver this feedback separately. Providing feedback on more than a few areas can make the recipient feel overwhelmed and discouraged and won't achieve the desired outcome. You should also have concrete examples of the behavior you are addressing and provide an example of the type of behavior you would like them to exhibit.

Although it may be well-intended, don't mix positive and constructive feedback. A Harvard University study revealed that when positive feedback was given during the same meeting as negative feedback, the employee felt worse about their performance. If you have positive feedback to deliver, do it and do it as often as you can but try not to only provide positive feedback at the same time as negative feedback. In the event you are providing feedback on their overall performance, like with an annual review, try to compartmentalize and deliver negative and positive feedback separately.

It's all your delivery!
You can say the exact same words, but your tone, context, and follow-up remarks can entirely alter the feedback message and experience. Your delivery as a manager is so important!

Both parties may initially feel uncomfortable stepping into the meeting. Whether or not the topic of the discussion has been revealed, it can feel tense. For your team to feel more positive about the feedback, try to diffuse the tension. Lighten the mood, tell a joke, or speak about something lighter. It can help ease both parties.

In your delivery, consider your employee as an individual. As their manager, you should know their strengths, weakness, and communication style and should deliver accordingly. A one-size-fits-all approach won't work, and you should tailor your delivery. You should also exhibit empathy. You can do this by recognizing any extenuating circumstances, offering support, and showing vulnerability.

An excellent way of displaying vulnerability is to relate to the employee by telling them a similar experience you have had. If they are struggling with time management, tell them when you experienced similar struggles and what helped you. A personal story is a great way to relate. Using empathy, you must also ask, "How can I support you?" and wait for a response.

Simply saying "let me know if I can help" is not sufficient. As their manager, you need to open the door for support as most people don't feel comfortable coming to their boss to ask for help.

Remain positive and supportive throughout the meeting.
It is possible an employee may initially become defensive or could blame circumstances or people. Do not match their negative emotions. Use your self-awareness and self-management to remain positive, optimistic, and supportive.

Use focused listening and have an open mind, focusing on what they are saying. To make sure you understand where they are coming from, rephrase, repeat and ask questions. Pay attention to their nonverbal communication as well, and adjust accordingly. Before concluding the email, reiterate the key takeaways and action items, including the areas you may be supporting them with.

Emotionally Intelligent Feedback Checklist
Refer to the following list before delivering feedback.

- ☐ Check-in with yourself and your emotional state before providing feedback. You must be in a positive mind frame and not angry or frustrated when delivering feedback.

- ☐ Ensure you are clear on the purpose of the feedback. Prepare examples and write down what you want to address. Limit feedback to one or two items, otherwise it will feel discouraging.

- [ ] Avoid mixing and confusing positive and negative feedback. If you can, wait to deliver the two separately.

- [ ] Ease tension and remain friendly and supportive. Acknowledge that it's awkward, tell a joke or share a story (be vulnerable).

- [ ] Be empathetic. Consider the employees perspective, personality type and communication style and tailor your approach accordingly.

- [ ] Remain optimistic and positive. Don't match negative emotions.

- [ ] Listen attentively and ask questions when you need clarification. Make sure you understand your employee and give them opportunity to ask you questions.

- [ ] Clearly layout the key takeaways from this conversation so they leave the meeting knowing what to do and feeling motivated.

Examples of Emotionally Intelligent Feedback

Employee-centric feedback is tailored to the individual, as each member of your team will respond to the same type of feedback differently. In the following examples, you will see how different personality types require different approaches to feedback.

Scenario 1 – Defiant and Defensive
When you move up in a company that promotes from within, this can quickly change working dynamics. In this scenario, you are the manager of an individual with who you were once colleagues with. This individual is older than you, with several years of industry experience. They applied to the position you currently hold, but it was awarded to you. This change in workplace dynamic has been difficult for them, and their struggle with it has been evident.

Providing feedback to this individual can be very uncomfortable for you and them. In this scenario, they become defiant and don't accept feedback. They feel they are more entitled to your position, and their ego has had trouble accepting it. You will need to break down barriers and do this by honoring their experience and wealth of knowledge by asking questions and feedback on specific projects. Show respect, and you will receive it in return. This person may need additional affirmation in the early stages of this transition and may require a gentle approach when providing feedback, limiting feedback to one issue at a time.

Scenario 2 – Disengaged
As a manager, you have likely experienced an employee who has become disengaged. Although it can sneak up gradually, eventually, the signs are too obvious to ignore.

This type of employee is doing just enough to get by, and their performance isn't what it used to be. They may also appear less social, not as happy, and you may find them taking an increasing amount of days off.

An emotionally intelligent manager will address disengagement early. Through support and open conversation, you can find out the underlying cause and help motivate them. Don't approach them and bluntly ask, "why are you disengaged?", instead try to understand how they feel about their current role and where they want to grow.

For some, they may feel like their growth isn't fast enough, or they may feel there aren't any opportunities available to them. You don't need to promote them in order to boost your disengaged employee's performance. You can, however, provide more leadership roles on projects or find out if there is a particular initiative they are passionate about. Just as disengagement can come from boredom, it can also stem from feelings of overwhelm.

An employee who has been under prolonged stressed may be experiencing burnout and appear disengaged. By asking open-ended questions about how they are feeling, you can provide the necessary supports to reduce the burden that can be contributing to their disengagement.

Scenario 3 – Declining Performance
This employee used to be great. They were your right hand and always on the ball. Suddenly their performance is declining at a rapid pace. They've missed important

meetings, failed to deliver projects, and engaged in conflict with other employees. When the change has happened too quickly and is in stark contrast to their usual performance, it is best to address it immediately and directly ask why. You don't need to run through every single action, as this can make it feel like an attack, but providing a few examples will be helpful.

You must then listen closely to their response and ask questions to understand where they are coming from. Display compassion and empathy and try to come up with an action plan together to help get them back on track. Remember, they may be dealing with circumstances outside of the office, such as a serious health diagnosis. Have an open mind and create a safe space for them to open up.

Emotional intelligence is imperative for giving and receiving feedback. It's a necessary part of life. As Aristotle famously said, "Criticism is something you can easily avoid by saying nothing, doing nothing, and being nothing." You and your team are doing far from nothing. Everyone is a vital part of the organization, and there will be some constructive feedback along the way. When emotional intelligence is used, feedback will improve performance significantly and nurture a more emotionally intelligent workplace culture.

CHAPTER 11
MANAGING DIFFERENT PERSONALITY TYPES

Workplaces are full of different personalities. A person's personality type will impact their communication style, workflow, and team dynamic. There are so many different personality types it can be challenging to know the names and scopes of each. Still, an understanding of the different personality types can help you respond accordingly.

When you understand different personality types, you can use your emotional intelligence to be a more effective manager and leader. This is because there are specific success keys to managing different personalities and communicating effectively.

How to Manage Different Personality Types

There are several different theories and definitions when it comes to personality types. One of the most infamous classification systems is the Myers-Briggs Type Indicator. This personality measurement has 16 different personality types, and they likely all exist in your office. Here is a brief summary of each of the personality types.

Analyst Personality Types

These individuals are often very logical, adaptable, and calm. When there is a problem, they are eager to jump in and solve it.

The Architect (INTJ)
These employees will be independent and private. They don't need a lot of management, and micro-managing styles can actually slow them down. They prefer to work a lot and focus on the task at hand. These individuals are confident, decisive, and direct, which can come off as arrogant to some of the other personality types.

- **Key to managing The Architect (INTJ):** When assigning work, provide a clearly defined problem, concrete timelines, and the tools they need to solve it and then leave them to it.

The Logician (INTP)
These employees are very creative, inventive, and intelligent! They also have incredible analytical skills and are often focused on data. Logicians are often very private and sometimes miss emotional cues. Although they are great at their job, they may struggle with workplace relationships and come off as insensitive.

- **Key to managing The Logician (INTP):** If you have a challenging project that requires a lot of focus – this employee will be a perfect fit. Pass along any intellectually stimulating work and let them work alone. It is also best to provide guidance rather than rules.

The Commander (ENTJ)
These employees are natural leaders that possess a great deal of charisma and confidence. They have an innate

ability to motivate others to work towards a shared vision. Their strong will can be a positive trait, but it can also make them stubborn, impatient, and agitated.

- **Key to managing The Commander (ENTJ):** If your commander employee feels you are as competent as them, they will listen. When providing direction, feedback, or recommendations, do so with confidence and back it up as they may question you.

The Debater (ENTP)

The Debater is the devil's advocate. This is the employee who speaks up in every meeting to provide a different perspective. These people enjoy a good debate and sometimes do it for fun, rather than achieve a goal. Along with their argumentative disposition, they are energetic and quick. This can be exacerbated when they are mentally bored.

- **Key to managing The Debater (ENTP):** These people require a bit of independence but not as much as the other Analyst personality types. The Debater tends to excel in consulting roles where they work closely with others and have a more flexible work environment.

Diplomat Personality Types

This group of individuals are compassionate collaborators that work exceptionally well with others. In an effort to not step on any toes, they can feel discouraged or afraid to speak up. They often have a great deal of emotional intelligence and take a humanistic approach with all interactions. They are valuable members of the team and spread positivity.

The Advocate (INFJ)
These employees aren't the most common and sometimes go unnoticed. This is because of their more reserved nature. Although they may be quiet, they are incredibly determined and decisive and are loyal employees.

- **Key to managing The Advocate (INFJ):** When providing direction, be very clear about the bigger picture you are trying to work towards. Remember they are private individuals, so be careful not to invade their privacy and encourage them to share personal details when they aren't comfortable doing so.

The Mediator (INFP)
These individuals are intuitive, idealistic, and imaginative. Often they seek out positions or tasks that allow them to use their creativity. Sometimes they can get too wrapped up in the creative elements of projects and ignore more practical details like data, budgets, and deadlines.

- **Key to managing The Mediator (INFP):** Similar to The Advocate, be clear on the end goals and the bigger picture, then allow them the quiet space needed to express their creative abilities.

The Campaigner (ENFP)

These employees are focused on making everyone's day a little brighter. They are the types that are often seen chatting with everyone around the office (sometimes to a fault). They are usually energetic, curious, and very friendly. They have great ideas and people skills but can find it challenging to follow through with the tasks they come up with.

- **Key to managing The Campaigner (ENFP):** As they have trouble with follow-through, they may need extra support and guidance to keep them on task. They are excellent contributors to brainstorming sessions but may struggle as project leads unless you help them remain focused.

The Protagonist (ENFJ)

These protagonists are charismatic and inspiring, which also makes them great leaders. They are typically very cheerful and friendly, getting along with everyone.

- **Key to managing The Protagonist (ENFJ):** These individuals thrive when working with others. They are great leaders and can help inspire others.

Sentinel Personality Types

These personality types love routine. They are creatures of habit and don't like when their routine is changed. The pandemic was exceptionally disruptive to these individuals and could have shaken up their workflow. They are dedicated and consistent, and you can rely on them to complete the project on time. Their dependability helps others on the team as well.

The Logistician (ISTJ)
These are hard-working individuals who are exceptionality organized and often exceed deadlines. They take timelines very seriously and become impatient with those who don't adhere to processes or meet deadlines.

- **Key to managing The Logistician (ISTJ)**: If they need your support or documents in order to meet their deadline, ensure you are delivering in a timely matter so they can do what they do best! As a manager, if you have established processes, you should also ensure that everyone follows them.

The Defender (ISFJ)
These employees are very practical, level-headed, loyal, and supported. If they are passionate about something, they will speak up. The Defender can be reluctant to change and can become preoccupied with meeting others' expectations.

- **Key to managing The Defender (ISFJ)**: The Defender won't ask for help when needed, so you should check in with them periodically and ask if they need anything or how you can best assist.

The Executive (ESTJ)
The executive loves rules. They prioritize honesty and hard work and will be the first to address any rule or process violation. If they suspect laziness or cheating, they will

become upset. These qualities can be great for leadership roles; however, they may also be too rigid and have trouble accepting that not everyone works the same way they do.

- **Key to managing The Executive (ESTJ):** They want fairness, and from their manager, they expect you to uphold the rules. If a rule is broken, address it and ensure all team members are treated equally.

The Consul (ESFJ)

These employees spread their positive energy everywhere they go. They love caring for and spending time with other people. They are sensitive individuals which means they may take feedback or criticism hard. The seek words of affirmation and frequently look for praise.

- **Key to managing The Consul (ESJF):** Be sure to let them know when they have done something well. Make an effort to acknowledge their hard work.

Explorer Personality Types

These are the bold, enthusiastic, and hands-on type of employees. They love learning new things and are very flexible, even when facing uncertainty. They are very easy going and like change. Explorer personality types are also very agile and able to adapt quickly.

The Virtuoso (ISTP)

These employees are rational, reserved, and calm, but there is a lot more than meets the eye. They tend to be mysterious and can also be spontaneous and take risks. This makes them unpredictable and sometimes blunt.

- **Key to managing The Virtuoso (ISTP):** The Virtuoso will appreciate a diverse, almost random list of tasks. If you or another team member has a lot on their plate, this employee is a great person to ask for help. They are eager to jump in and learn new tasks and are often very enthusiastic.

The Adventurer (ISFP)

These employees live in the moment and are often multi-passionate with many different interests and skills. They don't like to look too far into the future, making long-term planning difficult. They are often selfless and can put others' interests before their own.

- **Key to managing The Adventurer (ISFP):** Reward their spontaneous nature with new tasks and missions. New environments like conferences or attending a meeting on your behalf will be exceptionally rewarding for them. As they can focus on helping others more than themselves, keep an eye on them to make sure they don't experience burnout.

The Entertainer (ESFP)

These people crave the spotlight, whether it is asking questions in a big meeting or giving presentations. It's hard to get the mic out of their hands. They love to socialize and have great charisma, making them perfect for client-facing roles like sales. When working alone, they can quickly become bored and disengaged.

- **Key to managing The Entertainer (ESFP):** They love to have fun. Before talking about business and to-do lists, ask them about vacations or their weekend to give them the social aspect they need to remain engaged.

The Entrepreneur (ESTP)

These individuals are risk-takers. They have no problem diving into new challenges. They love learning new things and being social. They often want and respect fast change, which can cause them to feel restless and stifled in corporate environments.

- **Key to managing The Entrepreneur (ESTP):** Loop them in on the exciting and innovative initiatives the company is pursuing. They will be eager about new products and technology. They will also do a great job looking for innovative ways to do things within the company to make their job easier.

Everyone on your team will have a unique set of beliefs, goals, and working styles. It is rare to find someone who perfectly fits in the defined box of a personality type, but it can give you a better understanding of how they work, think and thrive. As a manager, you can be a more effective leader by supporting each team member's strengths and unique needs.

Case Study: Conflicting Personality Types
Scenario:
You paired up two members of your team, Lin and Pina, to work on a project. It is a long-term initiative that has taken about a year to complete. Lin feels like she has reached her "boiling point" and feels that Pina isn't communicating with her. Whenever Lin tries to check in, she feels like Pina is unwilling to provide information on where she is on the project. Lin has become extremely frustrated.

This isn't the first time Lin has become frustrated at work, especially when others weren't communicating with her enough and didn't want to talk things over. She would vent and gossip to other co-workers that Pina was shady and secretive.

Assessment:
It is clear there is a lack of emotional intelligence with both parties. Pina may not be aware that Lin is frustrated or ineffectively dealing with it. On the other hand, Lin is not managing her feelings of frustration appropriately and engaging in toxic workplace behavior.

Managing these employees:
Lin came to you, her manager, and expressed her frustration, "Pina is deliberately withholding information. I have asked repeatedly, and she always says it's being handled. She is keeping me in the dark, and I can't work like this".

To understand the whole story, you speak with Pina and ask her how it's going. She tells you, "Lin is harassing me.

She is overwhelming me with questions and continuously talking about silly details that I can't even think or do the work. She is bullying me".

Pina and Lin may be your all-star employees, but without emotional intelligence, this project is doomed. As their manager, you should understand that Pina and Lin have different personality types and working styles. If they don't understand these differences, it can lead to frustration – as it has in this scenario.

You hold a meeting and review the different personality types. You then help them use their own emotional intelligence and understand the situation from another person's viewpoint. This scenario could have been prevented by training your team on personality types early on.

Communicating with Different Personality Types Using Emotional Intelligence

Your emotional intelligence will allow you to communicate effectively with different personality types. Different personality types communicate and process information differently. For example, personalities in The Analysts group can have trouble communicating with those from the Explorer group, just like Pina and Lin in the case study.

Emotional intelligence will help you be more aware of your communicative approach and help you adjust your communication style, tailoring it to the person you are speaking with. This is why those with high emotional intelligence have high social skills.

As a team-building activity, have everyone take a personality test and then review the following communication strategies.

When communicating with ENTJ, INTJ, ENTP, and INTP personality types:
- Appeal to their intellect and give them a challenge
- Be well-reasoned
- Use visual aids, diagrams and charts
- Incorporate theories and complex concepts
- Demonstrate how the problem or project ties into the big picture

These individuals will find the following easy to understand:

- Future, e.g., outcome, how things and events may develop, consequences, future perspectives
- History, e.g., preceding events
- Review, e.g., analyst opinions, expert reviews
- Paradoxical facts, e.g., practices that seem to contradict established beliefs
- Assessment, e.g., estimation of qualities or value, analysis
- Trends
- Ideas, concepts

These individuals will struggle to comprehend the following topics:

- When there is no other alternative
- Subtle differences in feelings
- Gossip

When communicating with ENFJ, INFJ, ENFP, and INFP personality types:
- Use reason, but be expressive
- Incorporate visual aids (e.g., graphs, tables, pictures)
- Appeal to their intuitions

These individuals will find the following easy to understand:

- Teachings
- Casual chatter
- Personal appearance, style, or fashion
- Reviews
- Feelings
- Ideas
- Values

These individuals will struggle to comprehend the following topics:

- When there is no other alternative
- Extremely detailed explanations

When communicating with ESFJ, ISFJ, ESFP, and ISFP personality types:
- Be supportive and confident when speaking
- Provide concrete examples
- Outline immediate advantages, ROI, profit
- Appeal to their emotions

These individuals will find the following easy to understand:

- Guesswork and premonitions
- Practices, e.g., ways of doing something
- Opinions and beliefs
- Looks, e.g., way a thing or person appears
- Resources, e.g., money, material, equipment, means, personnel

These individuals will struggle to comprehend the following topics:

- Theoretic or scientific principles
- Analyses
- Facts that contradict establish believes or practices

When communicating with ESTJ, ISTJ, ESTP, and ISTP personality types:
- Be reasonable, clear and supportive
- Provide examples using visual aids
- Demonstrate the immediate advantage

These individuals will find the following easy to understand:

- Rules, e.g., policies, regulations, rules, procedures
- Practices, e.g., specific way of doing a task
- Implementation, e.g., ways of realization, how things are carried out

- Resources, e.g., equipment, tools, money, means, materials
- Analysis, e.g., study of interrelationships, examining data

These individuals will struggle to comprehend the following topics:

- Feelings and emotions
- Beliefs
- Casual chatter
- Guesswork

Using Emotional Intelligence in All Communication

Understanding different personality types will allow you communicate more effectively by helping you express your message and understand the person you are speaking with. In addition to tailoring your communication, you should always apply emotional intelligence.

Regardless of a team member's personality style, you must consider their feelings. If someone seems angry or just told you something out of character, consider why they may be acting like that and what their emotional state is. Their emotional state should then affect your response.

You must also consider your own feelings as they will affect the message you are trying to send. When you identify a strong emotion like anger or stress, you must pay attention to this and ensure it doesn't interfere with your message. Often we think of the negative consequences associated with negative emotions, but positive emotions can have adverse effects as well if you aren't in control of them. If you are feeling exceptionally happy at the moment, you could overcommit to a project or agree to a deal that isn't beneficial. Always pay attention to your own emotions.

Empathy is a vital part of emotional intelligence. It will enable you to relate to the feelings of your team. You will recognize and then understand their emotions. For example, if a person on your team seems stressed, you can ask them questions to determine why. Let's say this employee then told you they were worried because of competing priorities, and they didn't feel they had enough time to complete a project. As their manager, you can put yourself in their shoes and empathize with how they are feeling. You can then take this a step further and consider how they would like to be spoken to at that moment. Some individuals are looking for help and support, others want words of encouragement, and sometimes people just want someone to listen.

Good communication requires trust. You must earn the trust of your team members for them to trust that you are listening and care about what they are telling you. Your nonverbal cues must match the message you are trying to convey. If you tell them they can always come to you to talk, but you continue to write an email or text on your phone as they are talking, they won't trust you. If you are shaking your head no or yes, or look annoyed, it can also send a conflicting message.

Managing Different Personality Types

Being aware of your nonverbal communication, emotions, and the feelings of others will help reduce the number of misunderstandings, but they can still happen. Misunderstandings occur when you and another person think you are on the same page, but in reality, you are interpreting the situation or conversation differently. Misunderstandings are common, and they can be caused by differing emotions.

Strong communication skills are vital to the success of your team and organization. By increasing your emotional intelligence skills and learning more about different personality types, you will reduce the number of misunderstandings and achieve better workplace synergy.

CHAPTER 12
THE POWER OF EMPATHY

"Empathy toward others is the essential key to achieving high emotional intelligence".
- Robert Moment
ICF Certified Emotional Intelligence Coach

A few years back, Apple CEO Tim Cook addressed MIT's graduating class in his commencement address. In this address, he said, "People will try to convince you that you should keep empathy out of your career. Don't accept this false premise" (Zaki, 2019)

Without empathy, you won't succeed. It's *really* that simple. As empathy is a fundamental aspect of emotional intelligence, it must be a crucial part of your corporate culture.

Do you have empathy? Is it an essential part of your workplace culture?

To answer these questions, you must have a solid understanding of what empathy means. Empathy and sympathy are often used interchangeably; however, there are key differences, and knowing these differences will give you a better understanding.

Sympathy is acknowledging the hardships of others. For example, if a co-worker lost a loved one, you may say, "I'm so sorry for your loss," and feel pity for the pain they are enduring because of the loss. Empathy takes it a step further and involves putting yourself in the position of the other person. Using the same scenario, you may say, "I am so sorry you and your family are going through this. I know how much you loved each other. I am here for you," and perhaps making a meal and dropping it off, so they don't have to cook that night. Empathy involves a much deeper human connection and level of support.

Empathy pays off. From a business perspective, a corporate culture rooted in empathy will have higher rates of productivity and earnings, giving an empathetic organization the competitive edge. To receive the benefits, empathy must be demonstrated internally amongst employees, externally with customers and clients, and via all public communication and social channels (Parmar, 2016).

The 2021 State of Workplace Empathy study revealed that over 80% of CEOs see empathy as a key to success (Businessolver, 2021). This is because they know that empathetic workplaces have stronger collaboration, higher resiliency, and better morale.

Your ability to understand the feelings of others is empathy. This comes naturally for some, and others may need to make a conscious effort to develop it. As a manager, you can become more empathetic by asking more questions and *really* listening to the answers. Curiosity and observation will help improve your level of empathy. The underlying skill involved in empathy is perspective-taking.

It's your ability to see the perspective of another person. Perspective-taking will allow you to see things from the viewpoint of your employees, superiors, and the organization as a whole. It will also help you understand the challenges different people face.

Seth Godin, a renowned author, and entrepreneur has extensively written on the importance of empathy in business. On his blog, he wrote, "Gloating or silence closes the door. Empathy, on the other hand, and the action of speech, of moderation, of connection, can change everything. And if it hasn't been present before, it can start right now" (Godin, 2016).

Ask questions to understand how another person is feeling. Try and think of times you have experienced something similar and ask yourself, "How did I feel when this happened?". Focus on becoming more empathetic and leverage empathy within your team.

All leaders are involved in the creation of an empathetic culture. Identify the connectors and thought leaders in your organization and have them help champion an empathetic culture with you. With these efforts, highlight the positive effects of empathy.

The most negative individuals tend to be the loudest. This creates a phenomenon known as "phantom norms." When a loud employee is toxic, it can make it appear as if this is status quo. As a manager, you need to speak up against these phantom norms and ensure everyone understands that empathy is the majority. You can do this by recognizing empathetic behavior and recognizing your team members that display empathy.

Strategies to Create Empathy in the Workplace

Despite the power of empathy being recognized, many employers are not doing enough when it comes to empathy in the workplace. Recent research reveals that only 48% of employees feel their organization overall is empathetic. This 2020 survey found that empathy in the workplace has hit a new low when compared to the previous four years (Businessolver, 2020).

The pandemic negatively impacted corporate cultures in all industries, and a decline in empathy was one of these consequences. As a manager, you have the power to improve your corporate culture and create empathy in the workplace. Use the following strategies with your team to utilize the power of empathy.

Ask more questions

To be empathetic, you don't only have to be a good listener, but you need to ask the right questions. Asking the right questions will help you understand a person's perspective. When an employee shares a problem, respond with, "I hear you. What can I do to help you?". Your employees want to be heard and understand, and the easiest way for you to do this is by mastering the art of asking questions.

Walk in your employees' shoes

Each person on your team will have their own struggles, stresses, and responsibilities. Even though you are their manager, you must understand that you don't always have the complete picture of what their day-to-day looks like. This can be the root of burnout when bosses don't understand the full scope of their employees' job and continue to pile on the demands. Trust your employees, and try to walk in their shoes. If an employee seems stressed or frustrated, be empathetic by reaching out and asking how you can support, let them know that you "want to do everything in my power to help," and invite them to talk.

Acknowledge the feelings of others
No one wants to feel like a number or just their job function. The people on your team are human and have feelings. When stress and demand piles up, you may lose sight of this. Too often, employees feel as if they are easily replaceable and that their workplace doesn't care about them. This results in burnout and high turnover rates. Don't expect your employees to be on call 24/7 and to check all of their at-home stress at the door. Everyone has feelings, makes mistakes, and needs support.

Stay connected
As a manager, your job entails so much more than handing out instructions and providing feedback. It also involves a lot more than simply answering emails and offering short greetings. You must create positive relationships and get to know your team members. Use your emotional intelligence to connect with employees on a more personal level and get to know them.

Don't make assumptions
You must not jump to conclusions and assume the worst of people and their intentions. For example, if you have an employee who consistently shows up late, don't assume they are disengaged or disrespectful. Instead, ask questions and address the issue. If you catch yourself making assumptions about your employees and their behavior, stop yourself and speak with them using the emotional intelligence strategies listed earlier in this book.

The Emotionally Intelligent Empathy Management Formula ™
You play a critical role in the development of empathy in your team. Use the following acronym as your management formula to encourage and grow empathy in the employees you manage.

E = Encourage deeper dialogue for greater understanding

M = Maintain a calm composure

P = Practice the Art of Pausing before speaking. Collect your thoughts

A = Attitude of understanding and listening without bias

T = Take an open heart and open mind approach to listen and understand

H = Help by showing sincere concern and support

Y = Your ability to communicate and listen with your heart and mind is key

One in three workers leave their current company for one that is more compassionate - the power of empathy is indisputable! Your effectiveness, how well you listen and empathize with employees will determine if your team members stay or leave you for the competition.

Empathy isn't a one-time exchange; it's an ongoing practice that must be prioritized consistently. Use the strategies listed here as well as The Emotionally Intelligent Empathy Management Formula, and you will enjoy the benefits of an empathetic team.

CHAPTER 13
MANAGING DIVERSITY AND INCLUSION USING EMOTIONAL INTELLIGENCE

Your employee engagement and organizational success are a result of your workplace diversity and inclusion. Diverse and inclusive workplace culture is a shared responsibility and essential for the success of any business.

As you can imagine, there is a high degree of intrinsic value in maintaining a space where employees feel safe to show up and be their authentic selves. In order to create and maintain a diverse and inclusive workplace and manage diversity and inclusivity effectively, you must have a robust knowledge on the two terms and understand what it means to be diverse and inclusive.

Diversity goes beyond race, religion, and sexual orientation. It is the range of ways a person can identify themselves. This includes gender or gender identity, ethnicity, age, background, cultural experiences, and abilities. Diversity in the workplace is essential, but it is not enough for you to hire diverse team members. Diversity and inclusion go hand-in-hand. If your workplace isn't inclusive, you won't maintain diversity for long.

An inclusive management approach and workplace culture will build happier, healthier, more productive workplaces. In this environment, your team members will feel heard, valued, and respected. By managing diversity and inclusion using emotional intelligence, you will create a safe environment where employees feel more engaged and have a sense of belonging.

Benefits of Diversity and Inclusion in the Workplace

Managing diversity and inclusion using emotional intelligence is beneficial to everyone. To do so, you must have a diversity and inclusion plan that goes beyond diverse hiring. As a manager, consider how the diverse members of your team may feel. For example, if you only celebrate one holiday and not theirs, they may feel excluded and as if they are not an equal part of the team. You should leverage diversity and inclusion activities to create a better team environment. When your team is more connected, you will experience a thriving cohesive workplace in return.

With collaboration and cohesiveness, you'll also experience increases in innovation and revenue. Research has found that companies that have higher-than-average diversity also have 19% higher revenue (Lorenzo & Reeves, 2018). Other research found that highly diverse companies were more likely to reach financial objectives by 120% (Jacimovic, 2021). Further, diverse team members made up of individuals with differing races, genders, and cultures were better decision makers by 87%. These impressive stats are a result of the following benefits of diversity and inclusion:

Increased creativity and innovation

When you hire people from the same race, culture, age, and gender, you have a team with the same viewpoints and ideas. This is not good for innovation and will limit creativity on your team. When you have a diverse and inclusive team, you will encourage different opinions, perspectives, and ideas leading to more significant innovation.

Stronger teams

Potential new talent is looking for an organization that manages diversity and inclusion with emotional intelligence. They want to belong to a workplace that prioritizes D&I initiatives and work within a diverse team. You will attract promising new talent and retain your star employees in doing so.

Improved performance

Your teams' performance is a reflection of your leadership. When you promote diversity and inclusion, you make your team feel more engaged, happier, and confident. As a result, your teams performance will also increase, and employees will become more engaged and motivated at work.

The Relationship Between Emotional Intelligence and Diversity and Inclusion

At the heart of your diversity and inclusion efforts must be emotional intelligence. Emotional intelligence will help you understand different experiences, emotions, and perspectives. By increasing your emotional intelligence, you can make your team and workplace more inclusive.

As previously discussed, one of the key pillars of emotional intelligence is self-awareness. When you are self-aware, you will see any biases you may hold. Unconscious biases can result in systemic problems that create a toxic work culture, especially for diverse employees.

Self-regulation and social awareness will help you identify and repair any conflict that could impact diversity and inclusion. It will help you find solutions that continue to foster a positive workplace culture.

Another pillar of emotional intelligence is relationship management. Emotional intelligence will allow you to strengthen relationships with all team members and create a safe environment where every employee feels safe showing up as their authentic self.

In the previous chapter, we discussed the importance of empathy in detail. Empathy is necessary for a diverse and inclusive workplace. Although you may not understand what each employee goes through, empathy will help you put yourself in their shoes and better understand their perspective. For example, if an employee on your team has expressed concerns regarding inclusivity, you will use a high degree of empathy and listen, ask questions, and provide support by taking action, finding solutions in the workplace and following up.

The more empathetic and emotionally intelligent you and your team are, the more diverse and inclusive your workplace can be.

Your Role in Building Workplace Diversity and Inclusion

Regardless of where you sit on your organizational chart, diversity and inclusion is your responsibility. Diversity and inclusion is not a one-person job; every employee and manager shares the responsibility of creating and fostering a safe workplace environment.

You can manage diversity and inclusion using your emotional intelligence. This may sound easy enough, but unfortunately, many managers are still falling short. A survey revealed that only 25% of employees feel their workplace diversity and inclusion efforts are beneficial (Nishat, 2020). Use the following techniques to ensure you are managing D&I with emotional intelligence.

Talk about diversity and inclusion with your team

You probably meet with your team regularly. Whether it's a weekly round-table, project updates, or catching up on Monday mornings - use these meetings as an opportunity to talk about diversity and inclusion as a team. This will ensure everyone on your team is doing their part.

When meeting, first ensure that everyone is on the same page and aligned on what diversity and inclusion mean. Research has found that different generations have different views as to what it means to be diverse; younger generations view diversity as being cognitively diverse, while older generations view diversity as being diverse in religion, race, and gender (Christie Smith). Your team must understand that diversity includes a broad range of differences, including physical and cognitive abilities, race, background, and experience.

As a leader, you must be transparent and engage everyone in your D&I initiatives and activities, ensuring everyone understands them and has the opportunity to contribute and provide feedback. If you have a large team, you can create a small focus group consisting of diverse employees to help identify more options and solutions. That said, it should not be diverse employees' responsibility to manage diversity and inclusion. It must be entirely voluntary with no pressure attached.

A working group consisting of diverse employees, as defined above, will help you identify where you are missing the mark and what needs to change. It will also help you come up with solutions that will work for all individuals.

Ensure all members of your team take part in D&I training
You don't need to host the training yourself but should ensure that everyone on your team completes diversity and inclusion training. Training should be completed at least once a year and must be effective. Simply checking a box won't be good enough. It should be current and updated regularly.

Make your polices and expectations inclusive
Do you let your team leave early on certain religious holidays but not others? That is not very inclusive. If in your scope, you could revise policies to consist of floating

holidays that employees can use on holidays of the employees choosing. Use your self-awareness and consider the things you do as a manager that may not be as inclusive as they should be.

Hiring practices, work schedules, and expectations must be considerate of all employees. You must conduct an audit of your policies and expectations and try to put yourself in your employees' shoes – how do they feel? If your policies and expectations are inconsistent with the workplace environment you are trying to create, your efforts won't achieve the desired results.

Create a diversity calendar

All religious and cultural holidays should be recognized and celebrated. Not only will this create a more inclusive environment, but it can boost morale and make your workplace a lot more fun. You can create an online diversity calendar for your team and have members enter their holidays of cultural or religious importance. Then you, as a manager, can create the opportunities to celebrate and recognize these holidays from Christmas to Diwali and everything in between.

Organize a potluck lunch

A fun way to learn about each other is food! Everyone loves trying new cuisines, and what better way than to share them together? Organize a potluck lunch where people bring in their favorite dish that represents their culture. It is a great way to connect and learn about diverse backgrounds in the workplace. You can also use your emotional intelligence to make adjustments to the office kitchen, such as a Kosher refrigerator and offering a variety of different foods and beverages at work functions.

Advocate for inclusive employee benefits
Generally, employee benefits are a Human Resources function. Still, you may find a member of your team cannot take advantage of company benefits as they are not inclusive. This employee may not feel comfortable speaking up and could even feel as if their job is in jeopardy if they do. Use your emotional intelligence here and ensure all employee benefits are fair to everyone. This includes health benefits, time-off, and financial benefits.

As mentioned previously, you cannot enact diversity in the workplace in a silo. All teams and departments within your organization must review, enforce, and promote diversity and inclusion in the workplace.

Ensure everyone feels heard
To be considered genuinely diverse and inclusive, every employee should feel heard regardless of their age, gender, race, religion, sexual orientation, physical conditions, cultural background, or country of origin. They should feel safe and comfortable to speak up, especially if they feel there was any form of discrimination. A reporting system or an open-door policy will encourage your team members to speak up. When they come to you, use your emotional intelligence, so they feel heard.

Managing Diversity and Inclusion Using Emotional Intelligence

Emotional intelligence and workplace diversity and inclusion create a successful work culture with employee peak performance. Managing diversity and inclusion using emotional intelligence is critical to fostering a more positive workplace. By taking action and leading with emotional intelligence, you will facilitate mutual understanding and respect, your team will become more engaged, and you will benefit significantly.

CHAPTER 14
HANDLING SENSITIVE WORKPLACE COMMUNICATION AND SITUATIONS

As a manager you are bound to encounter sensitive scenarios where your emotional intelligence and communication may be challenged. Sensitive topics will come up, and they won't necessarily be related to work. How you handle them will determine your effectiveness as a leader.

Your team is your best asset, and they must be treated accordingly. If you are trusted, your employees may see you as a trusted confidant and come to you for advice or support. In some cases, you may find an employee from another team outside of the chain of command comes to talk with you. Sensitive topics like conflict with a co-worker, personal issues, or issues with a manager may be presented to you. Or, it could involve much more personal issues like a custody battle or perhaps they are at risk of losing their home.

Effective communication is critical to handling sensitive situations. If a person came up to you, and disclosed that they were sexually harassed at work, how would you handle it? You have policies in place but the way you communicate and handle the situation in that moment may not be scripted out in your company handbook.

To deal with sensitive issues, remember the following steps:

- **Listen and display emotional intelligence and empathy.** The employee has opened up and become vulnerable. You must make them feel comfortable and safe by listening intently and being empathetic. Make eye contact, focus on what they are saying and remain attentive.

- **Ask the right questions.** When an employee is opening up about a sensitive issue, they don't want to be met with interrogation but a key part of listening is asking questions. Effectively ask questions, when appropriate, so you can better understand the issue. Gather the data you need to make an appropriate decision on next steps, including how you will respond.

- **Provide guidance, if appropriate.** This person has chosen you to open up to about this sensitive issue. You are a person of authority, in a leadership role, and they may expect you to take action. Whether that is bringing a topic forward or providing advice it can be challenging. It's important that you navigate this step carefully. Show you are in control while continuously exhibiting compassion.

With the scenario addressed above, the employee comes to you with a sensitive issue. There will also be circumstances where you need to address a sensitive issue with an employee. Some topics such as personal hygiene, office romance or bullying may be tough for you to bring up. For many managers, these sensitive topics are much harder to address than performance issues.

8 Tips to Handling Sensitive Workplace Situations

When a tough conversation needs to be had, remember these tips to ensure you are handing each interaction with sensitivity and empathy.

1. Address the issues quickly

If you are addressing unacceptable behavior that must be stopped, you need to be proactive. Address the issues quickly before the situation gets worse. Sometimes waiting too long can make the conversation more challenging and could lead to potential issues like gossip, legal issues or formal complaints.

2. Prepare for the conversation in advance

Similar to how you would prepare before delivering performance feedback, you should prepare your talking points and facts in advance. Write down the reason for meeting, and all the details you may need for this meeting. Your nerves or an unexpected turn in the conversation could make it difficult for you to think clearly so its beneficial to have it written down. Further, documentation of the events, and conversation you are having will provide supportive documents if needed.

3. Brace yourself for different emotional responses

Even if you know this employee well, you must be prepared for a range in emotional responses. They could respond by crying, in anger, or become defiant. It is best not to make assumptions as to how the conversation will go. Depending on the nature of the conversation, it may be beneficial to have another person present such as a Human Resource Specialist.

4. Show you care
Through this book we have discussed the importance of emotional intelligence and empathy. When handling sensitive issues, you must show your concern and care for the person you are speaking with. Be vulnerable and let them know the conversation is difficult for you as well. You can also tell them how much you care about them and how much you value them. Lastly, focus on their behavior.

5. Maintain their privacy
Their dignity and privacy must be a priority. Never bring up a sensitive issue in a public setting or team meeting. Even if you think you are being subtle, it won't go over well. Schedule a private meeting to discuss sensitive issues.

6. Remain helpful
The employee you are speaking with may need help and you, as their manager, must be willing to provide support the best you can. A personal crisis such as addiction, depression or economic hardships can make it difficult for an employee to ask for help. If your organization has resources, help them get in touch with these support programs. An Employee Assistance Program (EAP) will often cover therapy and you could also help them access different support groups, legal help or books to get them the support they need.

7. Comply with legal requirements

There may be legal requirements surrounding the sensitive topic you are discussing. There are also some off-limit questions you cannot ask an employee and certain things you should never say. Familiarize yourself with this or it could create legal issues later.

8. Follow-up with the employee

To show you care, you must follow-up. As you wrap up your first conversation you should schedule a follow-up meeting so you can check-in. This will also help show you care and keep the employee accountable. If things are improving for your employee, acknowledge it and let them know their effort is appreciated.

Handling sensitive issues are arguably one of the most challenging parts of being a manager, but by utilizing your emotional intelligence and exhibiting empathy you can have these conversations respectfully and maintain a great working relationship.

Case Study: Addressing Hygiene Issues with An Employee

Addressing hygiene issues is a sensitive topic. Sal is a manager who leads a team of 10 employees. Recently he has received a couple of remarks about one of his team members smelling. Most recently, Sal received a call from one of their clients asking not to send this employee to their office again.

Handling Sensitive Workplace Communication and Situations

Sal has noticed it himself. In fact, it would be impossible not to notice it, but he doesn't want to upset or offend this employee. So how is he to handle it?

There are several things Sal should *not* do, like leaving hints such as soap or deodorant on the employee's desk. He also shouldn't act as the messenger for other employees who have complained about the lack of hygiene. Instead, Sal needs to address the topic tactfully and aim to minimize any feelings of embarrassment.

Sal asks the employee if he wants to grab lunch together at a local café the next day. This setting is both comfortable and private. It ensures that no other colleagues will hear the conversation, and the employee is less likely to feel attacked.

The restaurant Sal has chosen is usually very quiet at lunch. After arriving, Sal selects a table far away from any other guests. The two sit down and engage in a bit of chatter to ease any tension, and then Sal gradually introduces the topic by saying there is something sensitive he wants to discuss. He then tells the employee that what he is about to say may cause offense, so if he isn't in a good place to hear this right now, that is okay.

The employee urges Sal to go ahead, and share. Sal says that he has noticed from time to time the employee gives off an odor. He understands the employee may not realize it and wanted to bring it to their attention. After sharing this, Sal reminds the employee that he is sharing this information because he cares about him and wants him to hear it from him.

Sal ends this discussion by asking if the employee was offended by what Sal shared and if he thinks he did the right thing by sharing. This reiterates that Sal did this with the employees' best interest at heart.

As you can see with this situation, Sal attempted to reduce any embarrassment the employee may feel while still being direct. He allowed the employee opportunity to share how he was feeling and remained empathetic throughout the conversation.

If this employee became combative, Sal would have had to explain that employees need to come to work smelling clean because of its impact on others. Alternatively, if the employee explained there was a medical condition that caused the odor, Sal would then thank the employee for sharing that information and assure the employee he would do whatever he can to accommodate him and leave it at that. When dealing with a sensitive issue like this, try and put yourself in the employees' shoes. Consider how would you feel then use that when approaching the topic.

CHAPTER 15
DEALING WITH TEAM CONFLICT AND TOXIC WORKPLACE CULTURE USING EMOTIONAL INTELLIGENCE

Perhaps you were recently promoted to manage a team with a great deal of toxicity and conflict, or this negativity crept up gradually, and you aren't sure how to fix it. Either way, emotional intelligence will help you repair your team's toxic workplace culture.

A toxic work culture can have dire effects on your team's productivity, engagement, creativity, happiness, and retention rate. Toxicity can show up in the workplace in many different ways, such as bullying, harassment, gossiping, inappropriate comments or jokes. Fortunately, this is something you have the power to fix. Using the four pillars of emotional intelligence, you can repair your team's dynamics.

Using the Four Pillars of Emotional Intelligence to Improve Team Dynamics

The first pillar of emotional intelligence is self-awareness. You must be aware of the role you play in your team's culture. If you have allowed certain behaviors to continue or ignored the signs for far too long, then you have contributed to the current culture. Leaders play an essential role in setting the tone for workplace culture and reinforcing certain behaviors.

You must also be aware of the workplace experience each team member has. Is everyone happy? Do they feel safe at work? Do they trust their colleagues? Is there a diverse and inclusive culture?

Sadly, workplace bullying continues to be prevalent in the majority of workplaces. A survey revealed that 90% of employees have experienced bullying in their workplace. Be aware of the signs and observe interactions between your team members to identify any toxic behaviors, harassment, or bullying that might be at play.

Managers can also exhibit toxic behaviors that have consequences on their team members wellbeing. For example, if you assign unrealistic workloads and expect your employees to work all hours to meet these deadlines. Ask yourself if you have contributed to this toxic culture.

Once you have a better understanding of your team's culture, you need to repair or manage it. This may involve new policies, training, one-on-one meetings, and looping in your human resources team. To make a lasting difference, you must consistently work to make improvements. You cannot let things go or excuse certain behaviors from specific employees. Listen to your employees and ask the appropriate questions. If someone comes to you with a bullying grievance, you must take it seriously and address the issues adequately. The employee must feel heard and be able to trust that you will find a solution.

Additionally, you must manage your expectations. Do you expect employees to be on call 24/7 and working evenings and weekends? This is proven to have adverse effects on one's mental and physical health and will undoubtedly result in burnout. Be reasonable and appreciate that your employees have a life outside of work.

Empathy will help you improve your team's culture. Social awareness and empathy are your ability to understand the feelings of your employees. With a high degree of empathy, you will treat your team members better and understand their various perspectives.

Do you have policies in place that would allow employees to report harassment or bullying anonymously? If not, you need to. Employees must feel like they have a safe outlet to report any unacceptable behavior.

If one of your employees on your team came up to you and told you that another member of your team (your highest performer) was bullying them, how would you respond? As the manager, you need to manage the relationships on your team fairly. There is a lack of collaboration and innovation on teams with poor working relationships. You must hold everyone to the same standard and enforce policies fairly. If you don't, your workplace culture will only worsen.

Strategies to Improving Team Dynamics

Team dynamics can appear to change overnight, or it may be a slow process. Significant changes in an organization can trigger a cultural shift with employees. When people feel threatened, uncertain, or scared, it can change their demeanor and the way they interact with one another.

This is what happened to many organizations when they were forced to work from home last year. A sudden shift to remote work changed team dynamics significantly – and not for the better. Many have found that team dynamics and workplace culture have declined since working remotely, and some surveys have revealed an increase in harassment and bullying. To prevent this from happening to your team, use the following strategies in the office or remotely to improve team dynamics.

Touch base with employees individually and regularly
If the only time employees can speak to you is in a group setting, you are much less likely to find out about any issues going on. This is especially true when you are relying on virtual communication like video conferencing and email. Don't wait for your employees to come to you. Schedule some one-on-one time to check in and ask them how they are doing.

Host team-building events and exercises
You will find several team-building exercises in the final chapters of this book that will help improve teamwork as well as emotional intelligence. If you can, hosting fun events away from the office can be a great way to strengthen relationships, boost teamwork and engagement. Engaging in an outdoor activity or going out to eat is a great option. If you are working remotely, you can schedule a virtual happy hour or have lunch together via video conferencing, where you talk and get to one another on a more personal level.

Manage your expectations

It's important to reiterate the vital role you play in your team dynamics. As a manager, you are able to adjust your own expectations and demands to ensure some employees are not disproportionately affected. You must not expect everyone to have the same resources at home. Provide employees with the tools they need and manage your expectations.

Maintain boundaries

This is tied to expectations but is so important it needed to be addressed independently. It has become so easy for us to shoot off an email or send a text whenever something comes up. As a result, the boundary between work and home life has been blurred. This is a critical boundary to maintain. Countless research has shown that employees are more productive, engaged, and creative when they are able to unplug and rest. Ensure you respect your employees' homelife boundaries and give them time to disconnect when they are not at work. Unless urgent, try to hold off on sending emails and messages after office hours to set an example.

Continuously train and develop your team

All of your team members should be given the same opportunities to grow and develop. When work gets busy, or you are preoccupied with other projects, growth opportunities tend to fall to the side. Ongoing training, mentorship, and development opportunities like conferences are critical to keeping employees motivated. Your emotionally intelligent team members are less motivated by extrinsic values such as salary and benefits; instead, they are intrinsically motivated and looking to grow and improve. Ask each team member if there is any training or opportunities for growth they are interested in pursuing and help make it happen.

Emotional intelligence is the key to dealing with team conflict and toxic workplace culture. If your team isn't working as collaboratively as they should or, even worse, feels unsafe or unhappy at work, you must use the four pillars of emotional intelligence and take steps to improve it. With consistent effort and empathy, you can repair a toxic team dynamic.

CHAPTER 16
COMMUNICATING WITH FLEXIBILITY AND AUTHENTICITY

Workplace conflict, mistakes, missed deadlines, and tension is often a result of poor communication. Misunderstandings and miscommunication happen, especially as more people are working from home and communicating across multiple channels.

Leaders who communicate with flexibility and authenticity understand that they must tailor their communication to the person they are speaking with. Flexible communication involves changing your communication style to suit your audience.

The people you find it easiest to communicate with are often those who share the same communication style as you. Those you have difficulty communicating with have a different style. By being more flexible, you will reduce the number of misunderstandings.

Communicating with Different Communication Styles

In a diverse and inclusive work environment, you are going to be working with people with different communication styles. Meet others where they are while remaining authentic by using the following guidance:

- If the person is fast-paced and enthusiastic, communicate by giving them the bigger picture.
- If the person is warm, empathetic, and caring, communicate by explaining how the proposal or new policy will benefit the team as a whole.
- If the person is more reserved, communicate by describing in detail.
- If the person is fast-paced and stoic, communicate by delivering your message quickly and clearly.

This has become more challenging in a remote-work setting and now involves being flexible with the means of communication as well. Some employees may prefer to communicate via email, others may prefer an internal chat, and some may prefer to speak over the phone. Discover how your employees prefer to communicate and accommodate.

The Importance of Authentic Communication

Being flexible and changing your communication style does not mean you are no longer authentic. Your message remains the same, but you are positioning it in a way that the other person will hear.

Authentic communication is clear and easy to understand. It is vital to effective teamwork and strong workplace culture. Authentic communication doesn't mean blurting out exactly what you are feeling or whatever you want at the moment. That is not effective communication.

Effective communication is a two-way street and entails emotional intelligence.

Tips to Communicating with Flexibility and Authenticity

There are critical elements to communicating with flexibility and authenticity. Use the following tips to communicate more effectively.

Listen Intently
When you are communicating, you need to listen intently and focus your attention on the speaker.

Hold yourself accountable
It is your responsibility to ensure your message is fully understood by the person you are speaking with.

Prioritize clarity
Use clear, concise language and avoid ambiguous, technical, or specialist language to prevent misunderstandings.

Be honest
Being authentic means telling the truth yet remaining tactful. Don't tell people things simply because you believe that's what they want to hear. False promises or misplaced assumptions will inevitably break down communication.

Know the difference between opinion and fact
It's important to acknowledge the difference between opinion and fact and clarify when you are stating one versus the

others. Prioritize facts and don't make assumptions. If you need clarification, ask for it.

Remain consistent
Be consistent with your word and actions, and make sure the two match up. Stay true to your word by always doing what you say you will do.

Establish a connection
Communication will flow better when you have a connection with the person you are speaking with. Use your emotional intelligence and show the person you care about them.

Increase your self-awareness
The more self-aware you are, the better your communication will be. You must be aware of any prejudices or judgments you have that could get in the way of your communication. Further, pay attention to your emotional triggers and moods.

Flexible and authentic communication will benefit you and your team. Your emotional intelligence will help create better relationships, manage conflict and reduce misunderstandings.

CHAPTER 17
INDIVIDUAL EMOTIONAL
INTELLIGENCE EXERCISES

Emotional intelligence enables you to understand the impact of your actions, effectively respond to others and manage stress. The exercises in this chapter are to be completed independently. They are design to increase your self-awareness and help you understand:

1. Your own emotional triggers

2. When behaviors are a result of emotion

3. The function of emotion

With this understanding, you'll be able to respond more effectively to the emotions of others.

Before beginning these exercises, complete the emotional intelligence skills assessment located in the Appendix. Answer the questions as truthfully and objectively as possible and then return to this chapter to complete the exercises

Exercise 1: Emotional Triggers
Understanding your emotional triggers is the first step in managing the resulting behaviors.

Triggers occur when a specific behavior, person, or situation elicits an emotional reaction out of you. For example, when you hear someone crying, you may automatically feel angry, sad, or anxious. Past experiences often create these triggers.

1. Look at the list below and highlight or circle behaviors that trigger an emotional response in you.

Passive-aggressive behavior	Blaming others	Nervousness
Victim mentality	Aggression	Anger
Crying	Worry	Whining
Hostility	High-strung temperament	Need to please
Silent treatment	Lying	Unhappiness
Sarcasm	Conceitedness	Manipulation

2. When you are triggered, your emotions and behaviors can be more challenging to manage. Look at the list of emotions below. Which of these emotions is most difficult for you to control? Feel free to add your own if they are not on this list.

Resentment	Grief	Impatience
Envy	Fear	Doubt
Hostility	Sadness	Guilt
Shame	Frustration	Anger

3. Using the information from the two previous questions, complete the chart below.

Identify 2 or 3 of your emotional triggers.	Identify your most challenging reactions/emotions to these triggers.	Identify what thoughts or memories contribute to this reaction.

Exercise 2: The Purpose of Emotions

Emotions, the good and the bad, serve a purpose. Many of our emotional responses are innate and essential for survival. When you feel threatened, scared, or anxious, you may move to a safe location, putting yourself out of harm's way.

Our emotions also help us communicate our needs and identify when there is a need for change. Let's look at this a little further with the following exercise.

1. Briefly describe a situation where the function of that emotion was useful.

(a) Think of a time you were *fearful* and when that *fear* served a useful function.
Situation:

Function(s) of the fear served:

(b) Think of a time you were *sad* and when that *sadness* served a useful function.
Situation:

Function(s) of sadness served:

(c) Think of a time your felt *angry* and when that *anger* served a useful function.
Situation:

Function(s) of your anger:

Exercise 3: Underlying Emotions

Emotions are complex. Sometimes you may experience one emotion as a result of a less obvious emotion. For example, you may feel angry, but this anger is a symptom of an underlying emotion like fear or resentment.

Think of a scenario when you reacted with anger and try to discover any underlying emotions that may have been present by answering the following questions. You can repeat this exercise in your journal using different emotions.

1. Describe a situation in which you reacted with anger:

2. What thoughts triggered your anger:

3. When you were angry, what would others have heard, seen or experienced?

4. What underlying emotions may have been masked by your anger? Examples include sadness, insecurity, resentment, or fear.

5. If you had recognized this underlying emotion right away, what would you have done differently?

Exercise 4: Identify Your Strengths

This exercise will strengthen your self-awareness and improve your overall emotional intelligence. Self-awareness includes knowing your strengths and weaknesses – *how well do you know yours?*

Look at the list of traits below. Identify 3 qualities that you believe are your strengths and 3 qualities you think are your weaknesses. Write these down in the space provided.

When you identify your weaknesses, you know where you can improve and become the best leader you can be.

Creative	Happy	Fair
Confident	Focused	Loyal
Curious	Caring	Leader
Calm	Goal-oriented	Funny
Hopeful	Happy	Supportive
Imaginative	Patient	Kind
Striving	Hard-working	Dependable
Positive	Humble	Spiritual

Individual Emotional Intelligence Exercises

My strengths:
1.

2.

3.

My weaknesses:
1.

2.

3.

Exercise 5: How to Work Through Your Emotions

Journaling is highly effective in developing your emotional intelligence. To get started, use the following prompts. These writing prompts will help you identify your emotions, triggers, and emotional responses.

1. Identifying the Emotion
I am feeling _____ (e.g. Sad, stressed, happy, angry)

I felt like _____

2. Identifying the Trigger
I was _____ (location)

I remember feeling _____

3. Identifying the Response

When I felt _____ (emotion)
I _____ (behaviour)

Instead, I wish I had _____

CHAPTER 18
TEAM EMOTIONAL INTELLIGENCE EXERCISES

As a manager, it is your job to create an emotionally intelligent culture and improve your team's emotional intelligence. Use the following exercises to build your team's emotional intelligence.

Exercise 1: Accepting Emotions

Complete the following activity with your team. It will help you and those on your team better understand and accept their emotions.

Divide the group into pairs. The pairs should be separated with enough space so that they feel a sense of privacy.

In their pairs, they will share an experience where they felt like a victim. They will then share how they felt in as much detail as possible and how this experience impacted them. One partner will share first, and then the other partner will share their experience. Allow 15 minutes.

Discussion:

After the pairs have finished sharing, bring the group back together and discuss the following questions:

- What did you think when the other person shared a challenging experience?

- How did it feel to share this experience?

- How did it feel to acknowledge your own emotions?

- Did you feel more at peace after sharing and accepting your emotions?

- How can you use this going forward?

Exercise 2: Making Eye Contact

Eye contact is an effective way to emotionally connect with others and better understand emotions. For this team exercise you will need a stack of index cards and writing utensils.

Ask the group to spread out around the room and imagine they are at an art gallery, then move through the following scenarios.

Scenario 1
Ask everyone to move around the room as though they are in a public space like an art gallery, not making eye contact with anyone.

Stop the activity and ask everyone to write how they felt on their index card.

Scenario 2
Tell everyone to imagine they are in the same art gallery but seek eye contact as they walk around the room. As soon

as they have made eye contact, they are to look away quickly.

Stop the activity and ask everyone to write how they felt on their index card.

Scenario 3
Everyone is in the same art gallery, but this time as soon as they establish eye contact with another person, they will pair up and stand side by side. After pairing up they are not able to establish eye contact with anyone else.

Allow a couple of minutes for this and then stop the activity and ask everyone to record their feelings on their index card.

Discussion
Have everyone gather back in a group and refer to the following questions to guide discussion.

- How did you feel during this exercise?

- How did you feel when you had to break eye contact right away?

- How did you feel when you could pair up after making eye contact?

- If you were one of the last ones to pair up, how did it feel looking for someone to make eye contact with?

- Was it easy to make eye contact with someone?

- How close do you feel with the people you maintained eye contact with?

- What dictates our eye-contact behaviors? Is this different in other cultures, societies, etc.?

Exercise 3: Circle of Support

This is a great team activity to promote cohesion, empathy, and support. It will improve emotional intelligence as well as team building.

Form a large circle with everyone in your group. Spread out, so there is enough space for someone to walk inside the circle.

Select one person to stand on one end of the circle. They will then be blindfolded and need to walk to the other side of the circle.

The circle of support will ensure the person in the middle safely travels to the other side of the room by communicating directions, warning of risks or hazards, and guiding them.

The circle will need to work together to ensure the communication isn't confusing and people aren't speaking over one another. Before conducting this exercise, make sure there are no tripping hazards or risks for falls.

Exercise 4: Praise and Recognition

This activity will show acknowledgment and appreciation for everyone on the team and is great for teams that know each other well. In our busy work lives, we often don't take the time to praise and recognize our team members, despite it being so motivating. And when people are praised, it's often brushed off.

1. Write the names of every team member on a small ballot.

2. Have everyone form a circle and provide each person with a blank piece of paper and then have them pick a ballot. They cannot choose their own name.

3. Instruct everyone to write praise and their appreciation for the person on their ballot, being as specific as possible.

4. Once everyone has finished, collect the papers and ask each person to stand up. Read the letter of praise out loud and then together, say, "Thank you [name], you are appreciated."

Discussion:
Follow up this activity with the following discussion questions:

- How do you feel after expressing your appreciation for another person?

- How do you feel after you received praise?

- Were you surprised about what you received recognition for?

- What will you take away from this activity?

Exercise 5: Same Experience, Different Perspectives

This team exercise is excellent for boosting motivation and understanding how experiences can be viewed differently by different people. It can also be a lot of fun with the right team dynamic. Participants will see how even the most negative experiences could be spun in a positive light, and two people can view the same situation differently.

1. Divide the group into pairs.

2. Ask everyone to think of a negative experience that happened to them recently. Something that is over and not ongoing. One person will tell this experience to their partner.

3. The other member will then repeat this story back to them but spin it in a positive way, highlighting all of the positive aspects of the experience.

4. Ask the partners to switch roles and repeat the process.

5. Following this scenario, ask how they felt about this experience.

Before concluding this exercise, remind participants that the exercise's intention was not to dismiss negative experiences and emotions. A part of emotional intelligence is honoring *all* experiences and feelings. This exercise shows us that everyone can have a different emotional experience and outlook to the same experience.

CONCLUSION

How you handle that sensitive issue with a co-worker...

The way you deliver feedback to an employee...

The innovative solution to your boss's project...

The way you inspire your team...

Your rewarding relationship with all your clients...

Your collaborative approach with other departments...

All of these situations are influenced by your emotional intelligence. To be an effective manager and leader, you need a high level of emotional intelligence. In fact, emotional intelligence may be the most critical skill you have today and will not only impact you but each member of your team.

Now that you have completed this book, you have the tools needed to reap the rewards of emotionally intelligent management – *but will you use them?* It's up to you to put in consistent effort to use the skills, strategies, techniques, and tips listed here.

Just as it would take time to strengthen your IQ, it will take time to increase your EQ. Initially it may require more con-

Conclusion

scious effort, but with practice, you will move to a place where you instinctively act and think through the lens of emotional intelligence and empathy. Lead with empathy, and you will benefit from high level of emotional intelligence.

SPECIAL READER REQUEST!

Thank you for purchasing and reading my book! I am truly grateful. I hope the content added value to your professional growth. I would really appreciate your feedback on the book.

Please go to my book at Amazon and scroll down the page, and click on the link "Write a Customer Review" and let me know what you thought of the book and what insights you gained from it.

Thank you so much, and to your continued career success!

- Robert Moment

ABOUT THE AUTHOR

Robert Moment is an ICF Certified Emotional Intelligence Coach, Trainer and Speaker who specializes in helping managers, executives, and employees achieve high emotional intelligence for peak performance and career success.

Email: Robert@HighEmotionalIntelligence.com

Visit: www.HighEmotionalIntelligence.com

APPENDIX

Emotional Intelligence Assessment

To complete this assessment, you will read the statement and then select how often this is true for you (e.g., Very Often, Often, Sometimes, Rarely, or Not at All). Put a check next to your response and after you have answered all of your questions, go back and tally your points from each question.

Your responses will remain private and give you a better understanding of your current emotional intelligence level.

1. I enjoy managing a team.

Very Often	5
Often	4
Sometimes	3
Rarely	2
Not at All	1

2. It is difficult to read people's emotions.

Very Often	1
Often	2
Sometimes	3
Rarely	4
Not at All	5

Appendix

3. I recognize my emotions as I am experiencing them.

Very Often	5
Often	4
Sometimes	3
Rarely	2
Not at All	1

4. I am told I am a good listener.

Very Often	5
Often	4
Sometimes	3
Rarely	2
Not at All	1

5. When I feel frustrated I tend to lose my temper.

Very Often	1
Often	2
Sometimes	3
Rarely	4
Not at All	5

6. It is difficult for me to focus on one task for a prolonged period.

Very Often	1
Often	2
Sometimes	3
Rarely	4
Not at All	5

7. When I feel frustrated or upset, it is difficult for me to move on.

Very Often	1
Often	2
Sometimes	3
Rarely	4
Not at All	5

8. When I feel stressed or upset, I know how to calm myself down.

Very Often	5
Often	4
Sometimes	3
Rarely	2
Not at All	1

9. I am very aware of my weaknesses and strengths.

Very Often	5
Often	4
Sometimes	3
Rarely	2
Not at All	1

10. I do not enjoy my work and do not feel fulfilled.

Very Often	1
Often	2
Sometimes	3
Rarely	4
Not at All	5

Appendix

11. When people are speaking to me, I actively listen.

Very Often	5
Often	4
Sometimes	3
Rarely	2
Not at All	1

12. I often ask my manager and those that report to me for feedback.

Very Often	5
Often	4
Sometimes	3
Rarely	2
Not at All	1

13. I regularly set long-term goals and review them consistently.

Very Often	5
Often	4
Sometimes	3
Rarely	2
Not at All	1

14. It is difficult to build rapport with my team and colleagues.

Very Often	1
Often	2
Sometimes	3
Rarely	4
Not at All	5

15. I avoid conflict.

Very Often	1
Often	2
Sometimes	3
Rarely	4
Not at All	5

TOTAL POINTS	

Your Emotional Intelligence Level

Emotional Intelligence	Score
HIGH Your emotional intelligence level is high! As an emotionally intelligent person, you experience great relationships and likely find others come to you for advice, solutions, or when they need a "good listener." Those with high levels of emotional intelligence make great leaders and foster greater emotional intelligence levels within their team. Use this training and your own emotional intelligence to make these skills even better.	56-75
MEDIUM Although you do possess some emotional intelligence, it's not as high as it could be. This can show up in the workplace as having great relationships with some colleagues and difficult or hostile relationships with others. You have a solid base, and with this training, you can boost your emotional intelligence to high.	35-55

Appendix

LOW Emotions, stressful situations, and conflict can be overwhelming for you. You have difficulty managing your emotions and understanding the emotions of others. This can make building rapport and office relationships difficult. With consistent effort and by applying the strategies in this book, you can increase your EQ levels and have a high level of emotional intelligence.	15-34

WORKS CITED

Urch Druskat, V., & Wolff, S. B. (2001, March). Building the Emotional Intelligence of Groups. *Harvard Business Review.*

Alison Robins, N. S.-A. (2021, March 18). *Managing Emotions in the Workplace (Employee's and Yours).* Retrieved from Officevibe: https://officevibe.com/blog/managing-emotions-in-the-workplace

American Psychological Association. (2017, October 10). *Best Way to Recognize Emotions in Others: Listen.* Retrieved from American Psychological Association: https://www.apa.org/news/press/releases/2017/10/emotions-listen

Balman, W., & Bruce, S. (2015). *Three Levels of Listening.* Retrieved from Global Learning Partners: https://www.globallearningpartners.com/wp-content/uploads/migrated/resources/Three_Levels_of_Listening.pdf

Bariso, J. (2020, November 30). *Want to Hire People With High Emotional Intelligence? Look for These 5 Things.* Retrieved from Inc.: https://www.inc.com/justin-bariso/want-to-hire-people-with-high-emotional-intelligence-look-for-these-5-things.html

Brackett, M., Delaney, S., & Salovey, P. (n.d.). *Emotional Intelligence.* Retrieved from NOBA: https://nobaproject.com/modules/emotional-intelligence

Businessolver. (2020). *2021 State of Workplace Empathy.* Retrieved from Bsuinessolver: https://www.businessolver.com/resources/state-of-workplace-empathy

Businessolver. (2021). *2021 State of Workplace Empathy.* Retrieved from The State of Workplace Empathy: https://www.businessolver.com/resources/state-of-workplace-empathy#gref

Carney, D. R., Cuddy, A. J., & Yap, A. J. (2010). Power Posing: Brief Nonverbal Displays Affect Neuroendocrine Levels and Risk Tolerance. *Psychological Science.*

Works Cited

Christie Smith. (n.d.). Retrieved from Deloitte University: https://www2.deloitte.com/content/dam/Deloitte/us/Documents/about-deloitte/us-inclus-millennial-influence-120215.pdf

Davis, S. (n.d.). *Assessing Your Business EQ Strengths and Weaknesses.* Retrieved from All Business: https://www.allbusiness.com/assessing-your-business-eq-strengths-and-weaknesses-2-10174312-1.html

Godin, S. (2016, November 14). *Emapthy is a Bridge.* Retrieved from Seth's Blog: https://seths.blog/2016/11/empathy-is-a-bridge/

HappyCamper. (2015, April 28). *Business ROI of EQ Training.* Retrieved from HappyCamper: http://happycamper.world/2015/04/business-roi-of-eq-training/

Henderson-Loney, J. (1996). Tuckman and Tears: Developing Teams During Profound Organizational Change. *SUPERVISION*, 3 - 5.

Huy, Q. N. (1999, April). Emotional Capability, Emotional Intelligence, and Radical Change. *Academy of Management*, pp. 325-345.

Jacimovic, D. (2021, February 25). *The Importance of Diversity in the Workplace - 20 Key Statistics.* Retrieved from What to Become: https://whattobecome.com/blog/diversity-in-the-workplace-statistics/

Lorenzo, R., & Reeves, M. (2018, January 30). *How and Where Diversity Drives Financial Performance.* Retrieved from Harvard Business Review: https://hbr.org/2018/01/how-and-where-diversity-drives-financial-performance

MasterClass. (2020, November 08). *How to Use the 7-38-55 Rule to Negotiate Effectively.* Retrieved from MasterClass: https://www.masterclass.com/articles/how-to-use-the-7-38-55-rule-to-negotiate-effectively#quiz-0

Momeni, N. (2009). The Relation between Managers' Emotional Intelligence and the Organization Climate They Create. *Public Personnel Management*, 35-48.

Nelson, N., Malkoc, S., & Shiv, B. (2017). Emotions Know Best: The Advantage of Emotional versus Cognitive Responses to Failure. *Journal of Behavioral Decision Making.*

Nishat, A. (2020, April 30). *How to Develop a Diversity & Inclusion Program From Scratch*. Retrieved from Remesh: https://blog.remesh.ai/diversity-inclusion-programs

Ovans, A. (2015, April 28). *How Emotional Intelligence Became a Key Leadership Skill*. Retrieved from Harvard Business Review: https://hbr.org/2015/04/how-emotional-intelligence-became-a-key-leadership-skill

Parmar, B. (2016, December 20). *The Most Empathetic Companies, 2016*. Retrieved from Harvard Business Review: https://hbr.org/2016/12/the-most-and-least-empathetic-companies-2016

Rampton, J. (n.d.). *7 Ways to Create Emeotionally Intelligent Teams*. Retrieved from The Economist: https://execed.economist.com/blog/guest-post/7-ways-create-emotionally-intelligent-teams

Siegel, E. H., Wormwood, J. B., Quigley, K. S., & Feldman Barrett, L. (2018). Seeing What You Feel: Affect Drives Visual Perception of Structurally Neutral Faces. *Association for Psychological Science*.

Strange, J. (2021, January 21). *Emotions in the Workplace: How to Deal With Emotions at Work*. Retrieved from Quantum Workplace: https://www.quantumworkplace.com/future-of-work/emotions-in-the-workplace-how-to-deal-with-emotions-at-work

TalentSmartEQ. (n.d.). *About EQ*. Retrieved from TalentSmartEQ: https://www.talentsmarteq.com/about-eq/

Trent, N. L., Borden, S., Miraglia, M., Pasalis, E., Dusek, J. A., & Khalsa, S. B. (2019). Improvements in Psychologica and Occupational Well-Being in a Pragmatic Controlled Trial of a Yoga-Based Program for Professionals. *The Journal of Alternative and Complementary Medicine*, 593-605.

Wiens, K., & Rowell, D. (2018, December 31). *How to Embrace Chance Using Emotional Intelligence*. Retrieved from Harvard Business Review: https://hbr.org/2018/12/how-to-embrace-change-using-emotional-intelligence

Winter, T. (2018, October 31). *30 Interesting Statistics on Emotional Intelligence*. Retrieved from DTS: https://blog.dtssydney.com/30-interesting-statistics-on-emotional-intelligence

Works Cited

Zaki, J. (2019, May 30). *Making Empathy Central to Your Company Culture*. Retrieved from Harvard Business Review: https://hbr.org/2019/05/making-empathy-central-to-your-company-culture

www.ingramcontent.com/pod-product-compliance
Lightning Source LLC
Chambersburg PA
CBHW060843220526
45466CB00003B/1221